Picking Up The Broken Pieces Of Life!

By Jarvis "Jimmy" Ross

Picking Up the Broken Pieces of Life!

A Story of Healing, Renewal & Recovery

by
Jarvis "Jimmy" Ross

Troutman, North Carolina

April 2024

Copyright © 2024 by jarvis "Jimmy" Ross.
All Rights Reserved. Use By Permission Only

Editor: *Jarvis J. Ross @ JJPlanter.com*

No part of this book may be reproduced or transmitted in any form or by any means, electronic or mechanical, including photocopying, recording, or by any information storage and retrieval system, without permission in writing from the publisher.

"The Scriptures quoted are from the NET Bible® https://netbible.com copyright ©1996, 2019 used with permission from Biblical Studies Press, L.L.C. All rights reserved". Quotes from other translations are noted at the end of the quote.

Ross, Jarvis "Jimmy"

Picking Up the Broken Pieces of Life (A Story of Healing, Renewal & Recovery)

ISBN: 978-1-7351195-5-7

Cover design by www.createlogodesign.com

This is a work of creative nonfiction. The events in this book are portrayed according to what is recorded in Scripture and are a combination of facts from life experiences about the author. Other than Biblical characters, no names, dates, places, events, and details have been added, or altered for literary effect. The reader should not consider this book anything other than a work of literature.

www.jjplanter.com

Ode To Spiritual Liberty

When I sat down to write this book, I looked at my past rejections.

Then repented of my indiscretions so that I could make some exceptions.

Exceptions to the ridicule of superficial perceptions.

No one deserves to be despised under God's watchful Eyes.

God sees our heart so it's not wise.

Tried in the fire to raise me higher.

But the higher I got, I found ridicule from justified liars.

Anger was not the recourse I chose to take, so I closed my case.

Now I live a life that's great.
JJ Planter

Now the Lord is the Spirit; and where the Spirit of the Lord is, there is liberty (2 Corinthians 3:17).

This Book Will Free You From Religious Confusion & Spiritual Misdirection & Put You On Track Toward Divine Destiny

CONTENT

PREFACE: *What's It All About?!* (7-11)

INTRODUCTION: *Faith Guides!!!* (12-22)

CHAPTER ONE: *The Story of Trouble!!!* (23-36)

CHAPTER TWO: *The Challenge—The Clash of Human Fate with Divine Destiny!!!* (37-48)

CHAPTER THREE: *The Battle—Human Fate Ends Where Divine Destiny Begins!!!* (49-66)

CHAPTER FOUR: *Progressing Toward Healing—Spiritual CPR?!* (67-77)

CHAPTER FIVE: *What's Ailing You—Healing From Pain?!* (78-92)

CHAPTER SIX: *Scars of War—Old Wounds!!!* (93-105)

CHAPTER SEVEN: *Finding Purpose—God's Pre-Ordained Plan!!!* (106-125)

CHAPTER EIGHT: *God's Plan—The Way of Righteousness!!!* (126-134)

CHAPTER NINE: *Down the Rabbit Hole—Running From the Problem!!!* (135-145)

CONCLUSION: *The Human Condition versus The Faith Condition!!!* (146-163)

PREFACE

What's It All About?!

Chapter Overview

The objective in this chapter and throughout this book is focused on spiritual wholeness that results in spiritual, mental, emotional, and physical health. Most importantly, it's about how we prosper in the things of the Lord. We will explore Job's trauma and troubles, and spiritual and religious conflicts that relate to common life experiences. Most importantly, it looks at failures as "falling forward" onto God's "grace cushion" to bounce back. It discloses some of the most dreadful crises of life and how we learn to fight back in the trenches. No one is innocent in life, so assuming responsibility for the problems associated with our lives is the key to a breakthrough.

Picking Up The Broken Pieces Of Life is about the character Job and his experiences that parallel our common life. It's for all people, Christian and non-Christian alike. It exposes the backdrop behind the catastrophic episodes that brought him to ruin. But he bounced back through his acknowledgments of his human error and was elevated by God beyond his expectations. His story is our story . . . And it isn't the typical "how to" "self-help" story. Rather, it goes into the traumas and troubles of common life experiences in therapeutic language focusing on faith in God's Pre-Ordained Plan.

It is written from the perspective of facets of a diamond which leaves room for the reader to disagree because we see life from different angles. No two people see the same thing the same way. But, when we put the facets together, we have a complete diamond and a complete picture of life.

It is an adventurous way to explore the commonality of human experience and existence compared to the life of Job who triumphed through tragedy. However, it's not about people, politics, or religion "per-se." It's about life! I "really" don't think you've ever read anything quite like this—a cross between a novel, and a narrative with a dramatic appeal. Oh, it answers a lot of questions about trauma and trouble.

In a real way, *Picking Up The Broken Pieces Of Life* is the story of your life, and my life, as seen through the life of Job. It reveals relevant chapters from our lives that tell the story of our successes and failures.

****

The initial and ongoing fears of Job may have been: What would the public think of his life regarding his troubles and losses, especially if they viewed those things as sins and judgment from God?

The Book of Job doesn't give a duration for his trials and temptations, but regardless of the timespan, he seemed to grow spiritually along the way. His fears of his troubles and trauma were aswayed and put at ease near the end of his trial.

Trials under God's providence have a way of severing our lives from the past. They tend to keep us from ever returning to the things that got us in trouble because of the pain and suffering associated with our past and leave no residue. Therefore, trials under the watchful Eyes of God can cleanse.

—*The Objective: Spiritual Wholeness*—

The secular idea behind wholeness comes from rehab or getting clean from what ails us. It is an external process that takes place from the outside in. Spiritual wholeness is an internal process that eradicates the spiritual influences that plague us, thus cleansing us from the inside out and affecting the soundness of mind, emotional stability, and physical health. Both are valuable, but much better when coupled together. In hindsight, like Job, our trials and temptations become factors to create the opportunity for our wholeness but require us to set our fears aside and acknowledge our role in what's happening.

Also, and practically, Job's traumatic moments and our traumatic moments and troubles become a means to help others overcome similar problems. Through the scenario of Job's life, we can learn the value of our testimonies, brokenness, and the effectiveness of broken people in the Hands of God as *Wounded Healers*.

****

Job was unaware of the cause of his catastrophic calamity, so he defended his innocence and integrity against his acquaintances until God confronted him from within a vision of a tornado:

And Job continued his discourse:

"As surely as God lives, who has denied me justice, the Almighty, who has made my life bitter,

as long as I have life within me, the breath of God in my nostrils,

my lips will not say anything wicked, and my tongue will not utter lies.

I will never admit you are in the right; till I die, I will not deny my integrity.

I will maintain my innocence and never let go of it; my conscience will not reproach me as long as I live (Job 27:1-6).

No one is innocent in life. We have all said and done things that were not pleasing in God's sight and that was offensive towards others. That's human nature without divine intervention and divine intervention isn't something that we need to wait on.

The Almighty never leaves the Throne of Heaven, except in the Person of the Lord of Glory (Jesus Christ) who came to earth to redeem humanity. (The Lord becoming the Son of God did not deny heaven of the presence of God because of God's omnipresence.) So, in simple language, God doesn't drop down from heaven, and serve our answers to prayer on a silver platter to solve our problems. With the help of the diagram in the *Conclusion*, we will discover that divinity resides in us in the form of the human spirit indwelt by God's Spirit. So, divine intervention can be as simple as yielding to the presence of the Lord within us.

Job's claim of innocence prolonged his healing and recovery. Healing (in the Hands of God) is a process and is measured by the timeline of our acknowledgment and confession. Then healing and recovery can take place. Once Job acknowledged that he wasn't innocent God changed his circumstances.

When God ceases speaking to Job from out of the vision of the tornado, Job disavows his innocence and repents (Job 42:1-6). Then, shortly thereafter, God turns the captivity of Job. Yes, captivity because we can become spiritual hostages. *"and they will come to their senses and escape the devil's trap where they are held captive to do his will"* (2 Timothy 2:26). Although Job was not captive to do Satan's will, some people today and even Christians who have been affected by negative spiritual influences can subjugate their wills to that negative influence. At some point, that stronghold must be broken or the person will continue on a downward spiral. The formula for breaking that "yoke" is repentance, forgiveness, confession, and in some cases, renouncing the influence.

—*Job's Trauma and Troubles were a Spiritual Battle*—

The question is, do we believe in a spiritual conflict that erupts into a spiritual battle? The good news is that it's not a battle between us and the devil. It's a battle between the Lord and spiritual forces that try to impede our progressive walk of faith. So, it's not as difficult as you think based on religious jargon and rhetoric that you may have heard.

Our victory in life is as simple as YIELDING to the presence of the Lord within us known Scripturally as the Light of the World that illuminates us, and our path. Yielding exposes toxic circumstances and toxic people. Then we are enabled by the grace of God to decide what and whom to remove from our lives. That becomes the prescription to see what matters most in our lives that sheds light on people to avoid and situations to stay away from. Then we will be able to "clearly" see God's Divine Design which makes us whole, thus, enabling us to *pick up the broken pieces of life.*

INTRODUCTION

Faith Guides

Chapter Overview

This chapter looks at the story of trouble in a troubled man's life and the idea that it could have a purpose that overrides pain and suffering. But Job had a faith dilemma through his trials that cleared up near the end of his trial. That is, his faith was mixed with religious thoughts about God that impeded and dimmed his understanding of "why me." His faith dilemma became his greatest struggle. Likewise, today, some who opt to claim they are Christians have a convoluted doctrinal dogmatic kind of faith that can confuse direction. There is a theological glass ceiling under basic "saving' faith that misconstrues faith as a means of getting things from God or using God as a shield for bad behavior. That glass ceiling must be broken to see your way out of trouble. That kind of faith that guides us comes from the "essentials" of faith.

D oes trouble have a purpose and if it does, what is it? Or, is it a dilemma wrapped up in an enigma? That's the reality of life in the Book of Job which tells a story— that I deem true—of the source and path of trouble. Let's call it the purpose of trouble which is usually a taboo subject because human nature is driven to avoid pain and seek pleasure. But we can't have sunshine without some rain. **So let's look at the story of trouble in a troubled man's life and the idea**

that it could have a purpose that overrides pain and suffering.

The Book of Job unveils many of the problems that we encounter and fall prey to at one point or another. So, this story is not just about the man Job, it's also about us.

Job's troubles are all-inclusive and there is no doubt that we will all face similar problems because of the commonality of human nature. Yes, we all can go through grieving the pain and death of loved ones; rejection; mental-emotional abuse, physical abuse; bankruptcy and financial setbacks; sickness and disease; failed marriages; abandonment by friends and family; betrayal; toxic-negative relationships; judgmental criticism; loneliness and isolation; depression; a broken heart; suicidal thoughts . . . "and the band played on." The latter is taken from the blockbuster big-screen hit, <u>The Sinking of the Titanic</u>, referencing the band playing while the ship sank. Sometimes in life, we can deliberately mask and downplay impending calamity that can be associated with anosognosia or the condition of denial. Are we taking our troubles for granted or do we see the signs?

> *Human fate follows the course of the demise of the world due to the downward spiral of human dignity and self-respect. It is a Scriptural and historical fact that we are slowly, from generation to generation, sliding down the moral ladder. The older generation defines it as getting wiser with knowledge but getting weaker morally. Maybe some people think that humanity is getting better and that's understandable from personal experiences. Nonetheless, our humanity is measured by how we respect ourselves and how we treat each other regardless of our "neutral" non-threatening differences. So, are humans getting better or worse?*

The decline in our social humanity causes ambiguity about God's imminence in the circumstances of life, thus affecting the faith perspective. (Is God in or out in this situation?) Nevertheless, every human being will be allowed the opportunity to encounter a divine purpose at some point that must be identified. When that happens, a problem arises that poses two choices concerning which way to go. We call it "fight or flight." But there are more than two choices when we are faced with trouble. The other choice is to wait and weigh your direction.

BUT, THE FAITH DILEMMA

Picking up the broken pieces of life **begins with "our" faith which is our spiritual eyes that can see us through our problems.** But all faith perspectives do not guide us through our problems. Faith is the individual's view of God and not merely their religious affiliation viewpoint. Everyone who's part of a religious organization does not know, or understand the doctrine of that organization. They affiliate with religious organizations for various reasons from family heritage to religious appeasement. But, note, this isn't a slam or slight against any religion. **So, let me take you through some comparative faith perspectives then we will look into how faith can move us out of trouble.**

There is a purported diversity of ways to God through various faiths and religions and we are free to take that course, so don't think I'm trying to sell you my view. It's about your choice. If there were three doors and only one would open to the prize, which would you choose? That's the way of a multitude of ways to the One God of the Universe. Or, maybe you believe there is more than one god. But, if there is only one God, only one door would be the right way. So, although we call it "faith," it's a guessing game to choose a door. It's like that for some people choosing the way to God.

Whether we believe in the God of the sacred text of Scripture or another way, we should narrow our faith to one door and one way and not be confused by different perspectives. It wouldn't be competitive and it would be easier and better if there was one door to the prize. **Faith in the Lord of the Sacred text of Scripture—Yeshua Hamashiach translated to English from Hebrew, Greek, and Aramaic as Jesus Christ—is neither competitive, difficult, nor optional.**

My "personal" faith focuses on "Yahweh" (Meaning Great Provider, Great Protector, and Great Guide—Exodus 3:13-14) known by different cultural names in antiquity and around the world. And, the incarnation of God in human form as the Messiah—the One who saves. But regardless of the culture or language of the person, faith that guides comes from basic saving faith called in the Koine Greek language "pistis," meaning to rely on another for salvation. In this case, it is Christ, our Lord. Pistis faith is not based on doctrine or dogma. Rather it is based on the teachings (Didache) essentials of salvation: The incarnation, life, death, resurrection, ascension, and glorification of the Lord.

In my estimation, God was manifest in human form in the Person of Yeshua HaMashiach; co-equal in essence, nature, and power with the Creator God, Yahweh. (Those are the original revealed names of God and the Messiah, not the translations of the names.) So, will God judge the religion of the person, or will God judge the person's heart? I believe that on the Day of Reckoning, we may be surprised about who enters the eternal immortal state of being. Let me continue with this for a moment.

Three branches of religion stem from Abraham, the Father of the Faithful: Judaism and Christianity trace their tie to Abraham through his son Isaac, and Islam traces it through his son Ishmael. The question is, will they be judged based on their religious perspective or judged from the sincerity of the heart based on God's Promise to Abraham? Again, will God judge the religion of the person or the heart of the person? (We will explore this question regarding judgment of religion versus judgment of the heart.) God is just and not fair in human terms. Here, God's justice is equal consideration of the heart.

We can affirm our faith and recite our assurance about going to heaven or the destination of heaven described by various religions. However, no one knows the depth of eternal life until we get there through the portal of death. Despite the teachings that we have heard about the afterlife, death is still a mystery.

Because of the nature of a complicated faith perspective in any form of religion, we barely understand the spiritual angle or the source behind our faith, let alone human existence (existentialism), and the purpose of the power of choice. Unfortunately, bad traumatic experiences in natural life can impede, disrupt, alter, or diminish our faith and cause us to doubt the existence of God because of negative human experiences. And, without God, where are we?

Where does our power of choice (free will) lead us through faith? (See the *Conclusion*).

****

In this modern age of the spread of the New Age, the faith perspective of people has become very murky, even among Christians. Christians who are not certain about what's being taught to them typically don't "buck" against it; even if they don't understand it because of fear of being seen as a heretic. So they dare not question the faith presented to them. **There are varying faith perspectives in Christianity and among some religious-minded people there are a plethora of categories of faith along a pantheon of gods.** It has become as complicated as it sounds. Faith in . . . has become like a multiple-choice question. We either put our faith in the God of the sacred text of Scripture (known as the Bible) or some other source. Because of the controversies in Christianity today, there is even a steady stream of seekers questioning the faith perspective presented to them, and leaving the Church for some of the following reasons. Let me digress for a moment to explain by setting the stage for the spiritual journey through this book.

[There seem to be conflicts and contradictions between what is portrayed about Christians in the Bible compared to what we see and hear today from *historical, traditional, institutionalized, Americanized* Christianity because of translation hermeneutics. (That's the historical evolution of the Christian religion.) It is obvious to the eyes and ears that there are diverse versions of Christianity as there are different versions of the Bible. I know it's a hard pill to swallow, but Christianity is the most divided religion in the world. (*"Estimations show there are more than 200 Christian denominations in the U.S. and a staggering 45,000 globally, according to the Center for the Study of Global Christianity"—*
https://www.livescience.com/christianity-denominations.html).

When we examine what they believe, each sect believes a little differently from the other but each slight difference divides Christians from Christians, meaning they avoid worshipping and fellowshipping with each other. Their faith perspectives clash. What's wrong with that picture? Tell me what that means about Christianity today. But, God is not divided and neither is the Body of Christ (The Collective Consciousness of Believers all around the World.). The Lord stated (In terms of Satan's deception and "reversed psychology" of accusing the Lord of "casting out demons by demons" in Matthew 12:22-28), that a "kingdom divided against itself cannot stand."

That theological phrase, translation hermeneutics, means translators have put their spin (interpretation) on the meaning of the copied text. (Although the original manuscripts of Scripture are inspired by God, translations are imprinted with the mindset and cultural perspectives of the translators. The original parchments and scrolls are purported lost or hidden in the Vatican called the Codex Vaticanus.) Let me explain it another way:

Translations only provide the surface of God's Word taken from the copied text that was transcribed and then translated. The "original languages of the copied text" go into the depth of God's Word and give the etymology (original meaning) of the text that some translations omitted, added to, or changed. Some of those changes in translations were cultural and have justified the atrocities of war-mongering: Advocating a violent God; dominating and oppressing indigenous people and rival nations through massacres for wealth, power, and control; even slaughter and rape; imperialism and colonization that seizes land and people, making them bond-servants or slaves; genocide; biased politics, and government mandates that oppress minorities, strangers, and foreigners, which is the opposite of God's command in Scripture. It has "actually" become a dilemma of mixing politics with Christian doctrine that deepens the social divide and is reminiscent of "why" Europeans departed East-European countries. They came to a new land that they called America to escape feudalism governed by the Church and the Crown through politics and religion. Thus, freedom of religion was one of the freedoms they sought, and now some Christian movements seem to be reversing the direction of the Founding Fathers.

Those historical atrocities seem to be highlighted in some Christian circles today (not all) and are being *vilified* through politics as the way of God that uses force, aggression, and threats; which seems cultic. What I see with that type of Christian movement is hate. And you know where hate comes from.

Something diabolical has crept into aspects of Christianity that I want no part of. This is causing an exodus because those justified characteristics do not reflect the character of Christ or His followers. There seems to be a void of empathy (known as compassion in Scripture) missing from a large number of those who call themselves Christian. That is the cry of those leaving the Church seeking other means of their faith that suit their fancy, which can be a journey of futility.]

My apologetic approach in defense of "saving faith" in Scripture is the God of the sacred text is not a hostile violent God, angry with "so-called" heathens, infidels, and heretics. However, those who rely on translations may see God as a warlike God. From their indoctrination of Scripture they may perceive God fighting for Israel and God did fight for Israel but not in the way that we may think. God's battles on behalf of Israel were more about protection than Israel violently assaulting other nations. However, we tend to misconstrue Scripture and fail to see that some of the horrific battles that Israel fought were a matter of their decision and not God's. That's the human element. Consequently, some may see God as an angry, hostile, violent, vengeful god. Also, they may see that perspective from the history of conquering nations like the Roman Empire and British Empire which used Christianity as an emblem of war.

Traditional Christianity has been marred by some nations for wealth, power, and control because of its worldwide popularity as a conquering religion but it is not the faith perspective of Scripture. In some regards, the nature of God's salvation plan has been abused and misused to control people. That's the nature of religion, not the Lord. So let's not confuse the image of God in the sacred text of Scripture with what we see in historical Christianity because there is a difference. Historical Christianity is merely about the spread and evolution of Christianity through the centuries. What we fail to see are the changes that took place in historical Christianity that drifted from the roots of the Early Church.

One walks on eggshells with the concept of an angry hostile god because they don't know the causes of God's austere anger. When things go wrong in their lives they blame their lack of faith and their "personal" sins.

That's not how the original languages of Scripture portray Christ and His followers. It doesn't help us to live a better life because it puts a dreaded fear of God in the person. (Fear in Scripture is not being afraid of God. Rather, it's about reverencing God from the heart.) God may be portrayed that way by some who support an austere version of God in Scripture. So, some may see God as a vindictive god using vengence as a means of justice on their behalf, then excusing it as the wrath of God to cleanse the land.

My initial thoughts about Christianity led me to embrace the faith that God reached people through love and grace, transformed our lives through the Spirit and Word, and gifted us with eternal life. I saw God from the pages of Scripture as the Author of Peace, not war or destruction. The point here is not me trying to make me right and you wrong. According to Scripture, in the forthcoming Kingdom of God, "who's right and who's wrong" isn't the issue. The issue is who's the bigger spiritual man and woman, willing and humble enough to reconcile our differences regardless of who is right and who is wrong (Matthew 5:23-24). The point is: Comparing the faith perspectives and coming up with what best aligns our lives with virtues that lead to a brighter better life if that's what you seek from God.

So, settling on faith in God is like navigating your way through a maze. It's either faith in an object like a vision board; faith in the elements of the universe and nature; faith in some charismatic leader; faith in what we imagine in our mind and the words we bellow out of our mouths; or faith in ourselves as a little god; or evolution from an impersonal first cause. Concerning the latter, I do not believe that a non-intelligent "nothing" can create the complexity of the universe, nature, the human mind, and the complexity of the human body. In my estimation, there must be an Intelligent Mind behind Creation.

[The confusing difference between Spiritualism and Spirituality may look similar. But, the origin and source will tell you if it's good or evil.]

Other non-Christian religions have different perspectives, so you see it's a multiple-choice question. The deciding factor for me that solidified my faith perspective was the following: Do they offer a redeeming Messiah who enters into a "personal" relationship with the person by atoning for our human frailties, shortcomings, errors, faults, and imperfections, translated as "sin" in the British language; cleanses the conscience, and transforms their lives from living the wrong way to the right way? You might ask, "What's the wrong way?" My answer is, "Anything that is destructive and disrupts progress toward a better life."

I draw my conclusions from the pragmatic viewpoint which outlines the sacred text of Scripture in *practical, understandable, relevant* terms as I point out a "down to earth" God. Although it sounds like it's making God conform to human standards (relativity), God is "down to earth" because of God's immanence in the immediate circumstances of life through omnipresence. God is never out-of-reach or unaccessible like a busy corporate executive or corporate pastor. Neither do you have to depend on others to access God for you? According to several passages of Scripture, the "Godhead" can be seen in nature (Romans 1:18-32) and stipulates that God is a practical God (not a mystical mythical mystery), within reach of all people. There are no elite people or believers in the Eyes of God. We may not be seen as equals in this world. But, in the Eyes of God, we all share equal status in the sacred text as sons and daughters and brothers and sisters.

Now if indeed there is one God of the Universe and not a plethora of gods, someone is wrong and someone may be right. That will be decided on the "Day of Reckoning" by the Eternal God and Creator after death, whether or not we believe or don't believe. However, regardless of what we think we know about death from religious teachings, death is a plunge into the unknown. Before death, the question for many is, "Who is the One True Living God?" Again that's your choice but please pray for the right choice because that decision is eternal. There will be no second-guessing. Atheism and Agnosticism will finally have an answer on that Day.

Most religions (as far as I know) believe in a "Day of Reckoning" and if that's true, we will all find out the truth on that Day. That was also Job's perspective. Because of the unknown cause behind his calamity, he states his dilemma and hopes in the same breath: *"If a man die, shall he live again? All the days of my appointed time will I wait, Till my change come"* (Job 14:14 KJV). In the interim of eternity, it is our choice, but make sure you also consider the consequences of religious judgment versus salvation and the restoration of life eternal. When put in proper perspective by comparison of Scripture, God's Word is not Judgmental and does not Condemn. That's the work of "holier than thou," "self-righteous" religious bigots. Although life after death seems far-fetched in our finite minds, just as we are moved to purchase health and life insurance, we should be just as concerned, or even more, about our eternal security.

Job's faith in the heralded Promise of God sustained him through his ordeal.

NEXT: *The Story of Trouble!!!*

CHAPTER 1

The Story of Trouble!!!

There is a parallel between faith and trouble. It means faith runs alongside trouble and is the key to unlocking a way out. The key is discerning your purpose and God's plan during difficult times. Once discovered, we will see that trouble shapes us in the Hands of God. However, we must discern the influences and influencers behind our troubles. An abundant life is a path and gift from God that keeps on giving and provides direction through faith that guides us to our destiny. But we must dismiss blame and assume responsibility for the identified troubles and trauma that happened. Blame is like complaining and keeps you in the same place. The key here is knowing that God builds the Kingdom of God within us through free will and the power of choice before we can effectively build God's Kingdom around us; within our families, and our community of service.

I've chosen a passage from the Book of Job to develop the parallel of his troubled life with our troubles. It intrigued me. It emphatically points out that although his life was riddled with calamity, distress, and disaster, there was a positive outcome to it all through his restored faith.

So the Lord restored what Job had lost after he prayed for his friends, and the Lord doubled all that had belonged to Job.

So they came to him, all his brothers and sisters and all who had known him before, and they dined with him in his house. They comforted him and consoled him for all the trouble the Lord had brought on him, and each one gave him a piece of silver and a gold ring.

"*So the Lord blessed the second part* (latter end) *of Job's life more than the first. He had 14,000 sheep, 6,000 camels, 1,000 yoke of oxen, and 1,000 female donkeys* (Job 42:10-12).

But a loss is a loss and how do we recover from losses when it seems as though it depletes us? Ironically, Job's life was even better than it was before his catastrophic episodes. But how can we pull anything positive out of a negative?

God Uses Trouble To Get Us Out Of Trouble And To Get Us To Where We Need To Be In The Divine Purpose And Plan. Without Trouble, We Would Never Get To Our Place Of Divine Destiny. The Key Here Is Knowing That God Builds The Kingdom Of God In Us First By The Virtues Of The Spirit And Then Enables Us To Build The Kingdom Around Us.

—The Parallel of Faith and Trouble—

He didn't think he did anything wrong because he lived in the lap of luxury. That is the man Job. The thinking of his acquaintances, who doubted Job's integrity (because it's human to err), and the populous around Job was that his loss of wealth was a sign that he was out of favor with God. God no longer approved of his life. But that's carnal superficial thinking that lacks insight into the perplexities of life. It's like standing on the outside of a house looking through the window; hearing chatter and vaguely seeing people in the house, but not knowing what's "really" going on. Then we assume the worst. Unfortunately, human perception is like laws that do not consider circumstantial evidence. It only considers concrete facts. So, even if you didn't do or say everything they said, you are guilty until proven innocent in the court of public opinion. So follow your gut and stay as far away from trouble as you can. But know this, trouble will find a way to you, so be ready.

****

Job's plunge into abject poverty and the absence of family and friends was seen as the end of his life. Well, why not, from the human logic standpoint? What use is it to live without someone who loves you, someone you can love, and things that bring comfort?

He was alone, yet he wasn't lonely because God was with him. **However, take note that God can be very mysterious and seemingly absent when we are faced with problems because God is growing our faith without seeing or feeling anything, preparing us for better days.** But how will we proceed to those better days without seeing or feeling anything that indicates we will make it?

He thought that God was on his side, so when things went south, God was blamed for his impending calamity and he accepted his fate as judgment for something he had no clue about. But God doesn't take sides. God is on God's side and radiates love for humanity created to represent the attributes of God's goodness, not evil. It's really easy to discern: Good improves life. Evil diminishes life. Good improves the quality of character. Evil corrupts character. Good elevates people seeking good. Evil downgrades and degrades good people. According to the scrolls of Scripture and various religious texts; God is good and the devil is evil. But the question persists among those who fear the unknown: What side is God on?

****

Trouble is an uninvited foe that terrorizes the life out of its innocent victims. *"Man, born of woman, lives but a few days, and they are full of trouble"* (Job 14:1). *"For evil does not come up from the dust, nor does trouble spring up from the ground, but people are born to trouble, as surely as the sparks fly upward"* (Job 5:6-7).

Like a wild beast, trouble ravishes its prey and feasts sumptuously on the remains of a torn-asunder life. It divides the carcass and devours it until, alas nothing remains. But faint not, for there is meaning in life, even in the midst of trouble. **When fate clashes with divine purpose, it produces a way out of trouble through faith.** *"Not only this, but we also rejoice in sufferings, knowing that suffering produces endurance, and endurance, character, and character, hope. And hope does not disappoint, because the love of God has been poured out in our hearts . . ."* (Romans 5:3-5a). *"No trial has overtaken you that is not faced by others. And God is faithful: He will not let you be tried beyond what you are able to bear, but with the trial will also provide a way out so that you may be able to endure it"* (1 Corinthians 10:13).

In the scenario of heaven, trouble has an assignment and job to do like a sculptor. The idea is to take a lump of shapeless hardened clay out of the ground and place it on the potter's spinning wheel to shape it (known as throwing) into something beautiful to behold. **Trouble Shapes Us In The Hands Of God.**

How Trouble Shapes Us

The information shared here may be new to the reader and some may find themselves scratching their heads because it's a hard pill to swallow and hurts a bit. But James Baldwin puts the restoration healing process in a hard perspective of mutual relationships. *"I think you owe it to me as my friend to fight me, to let me get away with nothing, to force me to be honest, to allow me to take no refuge in rage or in despair... and of course, I owe you the same. This means we are going to hurt each other's feelings from time to time...."*

A real friend will tell you the gut-wrenching truth and hurt your feelings because they know it is part of the healing process. Truth hurts but heals. It's like an oyster that produces a pearl of great price. When a mere grain of sand penetrates the hard outer shell of an oyster, over time, the oyster will attempt to remove the painful annoyance of the sand with an inner substance that produces a pearl.

Job's wealth wasn't the only thing at the core of his crisis. His problem with resolving the issue (sooner than later) was his self-righteousness. We don't know how long his ordeal lasted, but "he" lasted because of his faith. Nevertheless, his self-righteousness prolonged and prevented him from seeing his role and responsibility in the crisis. Remember, trouble is an uninvited foe, so it doesn't always mean you caused your problem. **However, taking responsibility for something is not the same as blaming yourself.** What did you do or didn't do that fed into the problem? Here's an illustration of my point from a pertinent example:

Typically, when a child among other siblings is asked to pick up some trash beside them in the house, especially if they didn't drop it, they'll "feel" like it's not their responsibility to pick it up. In their thinking, the one who dropped it should pick it up. Then suppose that's also the attitude of their siblings. So, whenever something is dropped on the floor, and no one wants to pick it up, it will accumulate a mess in the house. Imagine that attitude in a relationship where no one takes responsibility for picking up the trash. Are we thinking like an immature child when faced with "personal" problems? The house would eventually become condemned. So, the typical answer would be, "I didn't drop it." Then, the normal reply from the parent would be, "I'm not blaming you for dropping it. I'm asking you to assume some responsibility and pick it up."

Let me give you an example from a page of my life: I grew up without a father in the household. I got to know him in my teen years and saw a different side of him from what I heard from my siblings. I saw a good man, so I didn't understand why there was so much animosity towards my dad. He left when I was around seven years old. I wasn't a fly on the wall regarding my mom and dad's relationship, so I can't say either way "why he left." But I do know that responsible men and women will dredge through their difficulties to provide for their families, the best way they can. We see that in nature all around us. In retrospect, my mom or dad isn't responsible for the plight of my life. It was my fate. I can't blame them for my failures. Although they had serious problems, their problems weren't my problems. Like others, I may have been conditioned to think and behave a certain way because of what I learned in my environment, which is the way bad habits of the past are passed on. But I had my "own" unique problems unrelated to their problems.

I don't know my father's story, but he had his struggles and my mom had hers. Not as an excuse, but I think that the era of segregation contributed to their troubles that prevented them from doing better. So, I don't blame them for anything in my life. Rather, I thank God for my parents bringing me into this world and taking care of me the best way they could.

This is a story about four people named EVERYBODY, SOMEBODY, ANYBODY, and NOBODY. There was an important job to be done and EVERYBODY was sure that SOMEBODY would do it. ANYBODY could have

done it, but NOBODY did it. SOMEBODY got angry about that because it was EVERYBODY'S job. EVERYBODY thought ANYBODY could do it, but NOBODY realized that EVERYBODY wouldn't do it. It ended up that EVERYBODY blamed SOMEBODY when NOBODY did what ANYBODY could have done!

INFLUENCES & INFLUENCERS

To resolve a problem between people, sometimes we must assume (not all the responsibility), but some responsibility, which isn't the same as blame. Okay, what role did you play in your problem? Was it because of what you "did" or "didn't" do? Problems can be caused by what one says or doesn't say, does, or doesn't do, called omission and commission.

Although it appears to be self-exalting to put words in God's Mouth, as false prophets do, the best we can do is proclaim the practical application of what God's Word is saying. In the context of God's Word in Scripture, God's not blaming us for the problems that come our way in life. God's concern is our responsibility to resolve problems through a humble heart. God knows who and why. But God does desire us to recognize that we are all, in some way, connected, and one man or woman's problems can "influence" someone else's problem. That's the idea behind the "Body of Christ": a collective consciousness of believers all around the world through prayer.

Do you think that Eve (The Mother of Humanity who was influenced by evil.) was just as responsible as Adam (Representing Human Nature) for the fall of the human race? Or, was she excused in the Judgment (Genesis 3:16). She was also charged and judged by God. So, she shared some responsibility for the fall of humankind after being influenced by Satan in disguise.

Responsibility leads to accountability. Accountability in life is not the same as accountability in a judicial system, which is our dread of accountability. In our judicial system, it's about pleading "not guilty" or "guilty" to a felony or misdemeanor. **In life, especially as a believer, it's about answering to a higher authority and admitting your role and responsibility for things that affect your life and others.** That higher authority is God. If you don't want to admit it to others, at least admit it to God, and God will work it out in you.

We don't live in a vacuum. **We influence and are influenced by what we allow.** So, maybe we were influenced to say and do what we did, but did we allow it? If there was no indication that you allowed it, then your conscience is clear whether they believe you or not, and you don't have to defend yourself. The point is, concerning the results of a problem, the victim and the victimizer have a mutual responsibility to admit and acknowledge what led to the problem. **Does the influence that affected your words and actions excuse your responsibility or make you guilty?** Words and actions cannot be taken back in the minds of those who are impacted by them. It's like trying to put toothpaste back in the tube. The only alternative is to admit and acknowledge your role whether you were vulnerable or preyed upon. Don't blame yourself, but at least see your gullibility.

****

Life, sometimes, feels like a stage play, or better yet, a soap opera, which is why I think that so many people love soap operas and reality shows. Consequently, life appears as though we are all on stage, playing different roles, and acting out a drama. The Book of Job goes behind the stage, pulls the curtains back, and shows us the *writer*, the *producers*, the *directors*, and the *actors*. If you will the credits. Here, I'd like to introduce to you the producers.

There are two producers. The first is God Almighty and the second is the co-producer, Satan. Yes, God has given Satan a limited role to play in the production of life. That sounds dreaded, but it's not as scary as it sounds. **The role of the producers in this dramatic production of life is to influence the way humans think and behave (the actors) by delegating to the directors, spiritual and human influencers.**

Does it ever feel like God is playing chess with your life? If you have ever played chess, maybe you've learned that the best strategy is to think several moves in advance of your opponent. There are times when even a good chess player will do just that and make sacrifices early so it appears as though their opponent is winning. But the strategy and plan are they will lose in the end, checkmate.

Okay, in my extensive studies and understanding of God's Word, God "really" doesn't play chess with human life because God doesn't manipulate or tamper with free will. That would violate the nature of the Eternal Kingdom of God. (That Subject Is Coming Up) **But God does have a pre-ordained plan for our lives that we must discover.** In other words, sometimes it "feels" like we are losing at the game of life, but hold on. God is making strategic moves on our behalf that will give us victory at the right and best time.

[God showed me in my mind's eye what my life would be like from an early age, but I had to follow the divine road map. For me, that's the sacred text of Scripture. For you, it may be something else, but make sure it leads you to the right path.

There were directors associated with my life including parents, siblings, peers, and significant others. Some were positive influencers and some were negative influencers, but I did not allow them to define who I am. I've always been an "independent critical thinker."

I have an idea of where "free thinking" comes from. It's an Old Testament concept of "everyone doing what is right in their own eyes" which is the equivalent of chaos that abuses freedoms. I prefer the term independent thinker because it considers the views of others. So, my concern is, who's influencing your thinking and behavior?

Where I am and how I am today is what I "hoped" for when I started my spiritual journey. **But, the caveat is caving into fate and giving up on divine destiny.** If people don't find their identity through the stages of human development that I will share, they will have to make them up later in life. They will play catch up, or some will become late bloomers, which is why we have immature adults or experience a radical midlife crisis.]

Who or What is defining your life? The higher truth is we are, through free will, or what looks like fate. But an encounter with divine destiny can change fate.

Abundant Life—The Pre-Ordained Gift

"The thief comes only to steal and kill and destroy; I have come so that they may have life, and may have it abundantly" (John 10:10).

Here is an analysis (exegesis) of John 10:10 that describes the battle between our Lord and the devil for the souls of humanity. Yes, although that's a hard pill to swallow, it means that there are two eternal destinies, whatever we may call them. In my view, our decision to follow the way of the Lord will determine our eternal destiny.

But I do understand that you may opt for another way. The following words are paraphrases of John 10:10:

[In the words of our Lord, the "thief" is a reference to the first criminal of humanity, the devil whose sole purpose is to steal (in secret) the promise of God from the recipients. The devil's lying deceptive attempt is to distort God's plan as some kind of scheme or fabrication by men. One example is the lie told to Eve. It's an example of spewing and spreading that the Bible is a fabrication by men. His diabolical plan is to kill the promise by sacrificing or offering a substitute for God's promise (which is the work of the "spirit" of the antichrist). Then attacking the personalities who support the promise with lies and deception, thus defaming their name; and destroying their lives, specifically their influence. On the other hand, the Lord comes to bring "abundant" life. When the word is unpacked, it means a better "quality" of life and a "greater" quantity of life. However, it doesn't stop there.

A greater quantity of life is not about getting rich at God's expense as some have heard from the "Prosperity Gospel" adherents. **Prospering in the things of the Lord is about reciprocity.**

To "receive" the benefits of abundant life, we must "give" like "good stewards" managing our household, and investing when we can in causes for Christ that help people. It means giving to causes and initiatives that help people sustain a healthy lifestyle that meets their most basic needs by giving the Lord credit. That giving becomes a cycle that returns to the person with interest from God to continue the cycle. In other words, when we *give*, we *receive* and prosper exponentially to give more. NOTE: When you come to the *Conclusion* you will see that the law of reciprocity pays off greater dividends when we retire and need it the most.]

To understand God's pre-ordained plan for our abundant life, let me put it in the context of human logic and then look at how that logic applies to God's relationship with us.

First, as simple as it sounds, pragmatically, God's pre-ordained plan is God's plan for our eternity and is similar to our planning for a future event. We count the cost and lay out the plans and the results that we would like to see for our future events. If the results we want to see do not come to fruition, then we plan again until we achieve the desired results, that is if the plans are that important. **What's more important than life?** That's pretty simple, nothing is more important than life, regardless of how our plans turn out.

God's pre-ordained plan means that God, in omniscience, sees the future and lays out the eternal plan of salvation over time. The final results are reached through the free will of those who worship, serve, and love the Lord. Let's take a closer look at this as we conclude this chapter.

I believe that what is described as mansions in the Book of Revelation will be fully occupied with free-will worshippers in the New Jerusalem. In my faith perspective, New Jerusalem is the Kingdom of God on this renovated Earth (Revelation 21-22). Now that's the way I see the "gift" of eternal life, the results of our salvation through the Lord of Glory. You may see it differently in your mind, but let's look at some commonality of our views. Then consider reading through to the *Conclusion* for more details.

The intricate nature of God's Command is not "do's and don'ts," but is more like a Commission (Matthew 28:18-20). The Heart of God is Love and the heart of what

translators dubbed "The Ten Commandments" is also love (Romans 13:8-10). If we love God we will not violate those commandments because they are dear to God and intricate to the survival of humanity and the spread of the Kingdom of God through what has been dubbed the Gospel. But, note that we can't keep the commandments without God keeping us.

God knows that to make the Kingdom of God an enduring kingdom, it must be the choice of the Covenant Promise People referred to as a theocratic government. God rules through a theocracy, the collective consciousness of the people of God. God will be "all in all." *"And when all things are subjected to him, then the Son himself will be subjected to the one who subjected everything to him, so that God may be all in all"* (1 Corinthians 15:28).

God Builds The Kingdom Through Free Will: If the collective consciousness of redeemed humanity (through free will) was not in agreement with the sovereign Will of God, it would be against their will, therefore coercion, and eventually, there would be rebellion. It's just the way of human nature. If we adamantly disagree with something, eventually we will cease to support it and seek a way out. God doesn't program us like a computer. Neither does God break our wills like an animal to train us. **Consequently, and in the framework of God's pre-ordained plans, the plan of salvation to rescue, salvage, and redeem humankind from their fallen state was established in eternity. Then played out in time by Yeshua HaMashiach (Translated Jesus Christ) to redeem those who were willing.** Note willing. All who fill the "many mansions" will have followed the Lord of their free will. That's paradise! One of the glorious things that will make it paradise is what the sacred text of Scripture describes as an eternal "Family Reunion" with the Patriarchs and chief characters of Scripture. Yes, Scripture states that we will sit down with Abraham, Isaac, and Jacob in a reunion-communion supper. Accordingly, we will somehow know our new identities that will be given in a new name.

So, although death is a mystery, my faith perspective assures my conscience of where I am going. In the Regeneration, I believe that there will be a reunion of "blood relatives" within the broader Family of God who will know each other and occupy those mansions. God is "really" that good! Concerning those who may not be admitted into the New Jerusalem, the thoughts of the redeemed will not remember any pain, loss, anxiety, suffering, or question why. Eternal bliss will rule in a utopian world. ***"And I heard a loud voice from heaven saying, "Behold, the tabernacle of God is with men, and He will dwell with them, and they shall be His people. God Himself will be with them and be their God. And God will wipe away every tear from their eyes; there shall be no more death, nor sorrow, nor crying. There shall be no more pain, for the former things have passed away"* (Revelation 21:3-4 NKJV).** Just as God remembers sin no more, so will we. Our consciences will be wiped clean. That is the ultimate fulfillment of the Covenant Promise in Jeremiah 31:31-34.

The Kingdom of God will be on this Earth, renovated by fire that burns out all impurities (Revelation 21-22). Also, the atmosphere will be purified by fire; perhaps a nuclear blast that will not harm the redeemed of the Lord because of immortality.

Now that's the way I see the "gift" of eternal life, the results of our salvation through the Lord of Glory, and the goal of my faith. It thrills me, motivates me, and gives me blessed assurance that the life that I lived for the Lord was not in vain.

NEXT: *The Challenge—The Clash of Human Fate with Divine Destiny!!!*

CHAPTER 2

The Challenge: The Clash of Human Fate with Divine Destiny!!!

Like Job, we will all have a Chance Encounter that will challenge our faith to accept or reject the Lord. It examines how Job rebuilt his tarnished reputation and how it works for us. Fate can be defined as the inevitable, unavoidable destiny beyond our control that puts our lives in the hands of some unknown god. Divine destiny says regardless of the bad or good that happens (Romans 8:28), God has a purpose and plan to change fate. The greatest challenge to your Fate isn't any person, being, or thing. The greatest challenge to your fate is you.

Life itself is a challenge. Each day when we wake up we will face a challenge and whether we confront the challenge or shrink from it will determine our progression in life. Challenges stand between you and your hopes and aspirations to achieve your goals to improve your life. Do you meet the challenge in that context or do you shrink from challenges because you are afraid of failing or being hurt?

****

By comparison to the sacred text, it appears that Job worshipped Yahweh. Therefore, the book gives us peculiar insight into the ways of God, the ways of the devil, and the ways of man aside from the Torah, the five Books of Moses.

The Book of Job is considered by many scholars to be a true poetic narrative of the life of what can be seen as a "good" man who was very religious. *"There was a man in the land of Uz whose name was Job. And that man was blameless and upright, one who feared God and turned away from evil. Seven sons and three daughters were born to him. His possessions included 7,000 sheep, 3,000 camels, 500 yoke of oxen, and 500 female donkeys; in addition he had a very great household. Thus he was the greatest of all the people in the east"* (Job 1:1-3).

Besides wealth and religion, the book opens with a scenario of his character. Accordingly, he was a family man who cared deeply for his family. He also seemed to be charitable according to his regional reputation.

The "land" of Uz, where he was from, wasn't a city-state like we know today. It was a large region that encompassed ancient southern Mesopotamia, northwest of the Middle East, stretching possibly near modern-day Iraq, Syria, and Jordan. He was also from the Semitic culture, in the lineage of Abraham. According to some historians and Scripture, he was the descendant of Edom and the grandson of Esau, twin brother of Jacob. Given his wealth, prestige, and prominence, his reputation was known far and wide like royalty. Ah, but take heed. Once his ordeal became public, his reputation was tarnished. He was an affluent influential man, but when his reputation went south, he went down among those who admired and envied him in the religious community.

Please allow me to digress for a moment to share an editorial about reputation because reputation can ebb and flow. It becomes a question of the ebb and flow of public opinion whether people will like or dislike you.

Proverbs 22:1 says, *"A good name is to be chosen rather than great wealth, good favor more than silver or gold."* Coming from the Hebrews, a "good name" stands out from wealth and riches and brands you as a "good" person. The key to a good reputation is not public opinion, but your name associated with good character. Although Job lost his prestige, prominence, and wealth which represented his character, it was restored through his ordeal. The reason was that his reputation was not based on his wealth but on his goodness and generosity. In the end, he won the debate with his "so-called" friends. I don't think they liked him in the first place because he was a good man who exposed evil ways (Job 1:8 says he shunned evil.). People who envy good people don't like them very much because good people throw a wet blanket over their drunken enthusiasm by exposing their corruption.

[Within today's media and social media platforms; whatever gives "shock" value and "sensationalism" attracts followers and gains popularity. In today's society, if you are popular, you are seen as a winner and trendsetter. If you are unpopular, you are seen as a loser. And, just as quickly as you can become a winner, in the eyes of the public, you can become a loser even quicker. If you are seeking popularity, remember, it comes with a public price. To stay popular you have to continue doing what made you popular and re-creating yourself which eventually becomes exhausting. The Lord was popular and many people followed Him because of the material things He could provide. But He immediately became unpopular among the religious establishment when His reputation was tarnished by a Big Lie and He was no longer available to provide those things. He went from Winner to Loser in a matter of moments because the same people who praised Him put Him down when He could no longer provide things to back His popularity. They will crucify you! Ah, but note, the Lord's name (regardless of the language), representative of His character, was sustained throughout history, not only as Savior but as the

best man ever. Never back down from the defamation of your reputation. REBUILD!]

    This good man suddenly, without notice, and for no apparent reason experienced horrific disasters to his wealth, his health, assets, and family, and the apparent loss of his wife and friends, thus ruining his reputation in the eyes of those who envied him. The perennial question is, why does God allow bad things to happen to good people? Shouldn't it be good things happen to good people and bad things happen to bad people?

    One of the treasured truths of the Book of Job is that it opens a door to the spiritual realm and reveals the root causes behind his calamity. That is if we believe a spiritual realm exists in the universe. It discloses the *Acts of God*, the *acts of Satan*, and the *acts of mankind* in the face of problems that many of us will face. So here, I will establish the central theme of Job's life which can be applied to our lives:

When Human Fate Clashes With Divine Destiny It Produces A Problem Of Choice. Will We Run From The Problem, Fight Against It, Or Wait For A Solution?

—The Chance Encounter—

From a secular standpoint, fate can be defined as the inevitable, unavoidable destiny beyond our control. But what puts fate beyond our control are philosophies and theories conjured up from various interpretations of Scripture and the mythology of different cultures that put our fate in the hands of supernatural gods. That insinuates when bad or good things happen in life, they are in the hands of something (be it a law of the universe) or a spiritual being out of our reach. In simple language, it means that good or bad things were meant to happen like predestination. Now divine destiny tells a different story. Divine destiny says God has a purpose and plan to change fate. **So, here we are looking at the role of divine destiny in Job's life and what comes down to us.**

> *Now the day came when the sons of God came to present themselves before the Lord—and Satan also arrived among them.*
>
> *The Lord said to Satan, "Where have you come from? And Satan answered the Lord, "From roving about on the earth, and from walking back and forth across it."*
>
> *So the Lord said to Satan, "Have you considered my servant Job? There is no one like him on the earth, a blameless and upright man, one who fears God and turns away from evil."*
>
> *Then Satan answered the Lord, "Is it for nothing that Job fears God?*
>
> *Have you not made a hedge around him and his household and all that he has on every side? You have blessed the work of his hands, and his livestock have increased in the land.*
>
> *But extend your hand and strike everything he has, and he will no doubt curse you to your face!"*
>
> *So the Lord said to Satan, "All right then, everything he has is in your power. Only do not extend your hand against the man himself!" So Satan went out from the presence of the Lord* **(Job 1:6-12).**

That celestial scene with the fallen archangel, Lucifer (Angel of Light), who became Satan (Accusor, Adversary, Slanderer, or devil) through his attempted coup d'é tat against

Almighty God, takes place on the threshold of the postulated region of space called the *astral* plane and *causal* plane. The astral plane is shrouded by darkness. The *causal* plane is postulated by astronomers as a background of bright light that emanates from deep within the universe. Satan's approach to the Almighty stops there because Satan was barred from entry into the causal plane due to his insurrection attempt. It also stipulates that all celestial beings are accountable to the Lord for God's providence on the earth and in the universe because Satan comes among the "Sons of God." They were angelic beings giving an account of their stewardship.

So, know that any trial, tribulation, persecution, or temptation that happens in our lives is permitted by the Lord to strengthen the faith of believers, not to prove a point to the devil. When God sends us tests, God is unveiling our love for the Lord, so that we know where "we" stand. **(The test for Job was about his eyes being opened to know where he stood before the Lord.)** For God already knows where we stand but desires us to know too, as alarming as it may be to us when we discover we are not as close to the Lord as we think.

God never gives credence to any other celestial beings outside of the Lord. God is God and doesn't have to prove that point. We either believe or don't. So, if you are a Believer, how will you fare in your trials? Do you serve God for what you may get from God? Or, do you serve God out of love and adoration from the heart? But, know this, your proof of love for God doesn't depend on the rituals, routines, custom values, liturgies, or other forms of worship that you participate in. Nor does it depend on your charitable contributions; how often you attend church, or if you have been baptized or taken communion. I know that's a disappointment, but it gets better. **If those things come from the heart, they are approved by God. If they don't they will be lost in eternity.** Our favor with God comes straight from the heart "in spirit and truth." **The acceptable and approved sacrifices of the Lord in worship are a broken and contrite heart (Psalms 147:3; Isaiah 61:1).** Accordingly, even if you fail the test in your trials, it means you can bounce back through faith and repentance.

****

The accusation and argument that Satan raises is about Job and his wealth and that Job only served God because of the wealth that God provided. If God were to take it away, Job would cease to serve God. When we compare the evidence from Job's anxious nature about his fear of losing his wealth (gleaned from Job 1:5-6) and his fear that his children had sinned against God, Satan insinuated that Job, like all humankind, was selfish and only concerned about himself.

God accepts the challenge surrounding the life of Job, and Satan with limited control over nature unleashes storms and raids from rival tribes, as all hell breaks out. That slanderous accusation becomes the basis of Satan's argument against every believer in the Lord that will unleash trials and tribulations, and temptations to wreak havoc in their lives. The "good news" is, if the Lord permits and allows it, there is a purpose and plan behind it to elevate their lives, if they pass the test. If they do not pass the test, there will be another one. But, who wants to go through the same things over and over again? Know where you stand in your heart before the Lord. **This is where human fate clashes with divine destiny in the life of Job and our lives.**

Divine destiny is the ultimate place in life where we can make a free will choice. God works through free will to establish the unfailing Covenant Community of faith. Just as God's Word does not fail and is just as enduring as the eternal God, one's eternal security is perennial throughout time and eternity. That statement has nothing to do with the doctrine of Calvinism or the spinoff of Calvinism, "Once Saved, Always Saved." Our eternal security comes from the Covenant Promise made by our Testator, the Lord of Glory, Jesus Christ (Hebrews 6:9-12). That promise uttered by God in eternity is immutable (will not change), and is irreversible. So, if you believe that you have been "saved" by grace and have entered into a personal relationship with the Lord, the Lord will not change His mind about your salvation when you fail at any point; regardless of the state of your life. But don't get that statement wrong. It doesn't mean that you can live a lifestyle that is contrary to your faith and still expect to go to heaven. If you continue to live the same way you lived before Christ, it's an indication that your profession of faith wasn't authentic in the first place. *"Put yourselves to the test to see if you are in the faith; examine yourselves! Or do you not recognize regarding yourselves that Jesus Christ is in you—unless, indeed, you fail the test!"* (2 Corinthians 13:5).

Note here that a thorough examination of Scripture, particularly the Books of John tells us that when God's Seed is within us, we cannot continue in a consistent lifestyle of practicing "sin" that we sought to escape. Yes, we will make mistakes and some may fall into sin for a season, but because of God's nature (the Spirit) within them, they will repent and be renewed. **So know this, our choice for divine destiny can be shortcircuited if we make the wrong decision when human fate clashes with divine destiny; as with Esaau when he sold his divine destiny birthright for lintel stew (Pottage).**

So, remember, the choices we make in life can be eternal and those choices can be the most difficult decisions that we will face.

Job's decision to remain faithful to the call of God stayed strong throughout his ordeal, even though he wasn't sure about the outcome. He accepted his fate and because of his faithfulness, God changed his destiny from the fickled finger of fate and restored him with more than what he lost.

****

In my researched view of Scripture and life, human nature isn't essentially evil. But do you think human nature is primarily selfish and bent on self-preservation? Do we occupy the throne of our universe and are essentially self-centered? Is it "survival of the fittest" and "a dog-eat-dog world"? I think that's how we are wired upon birth. Once an infant exits the womb of the mother, the instincts of human survival kick in and the newborn baby cries out to attend to their basic needs. Do you think Job was selfish when he ritualistically sought to preserve his wealth and family and was that a bad thing? Was Job's mindset, therefore to preserve all that he had, and is that wrong?

Do you think something was wrong with Job and it was his fault for the problems that came to him? Did he "sin" and are all our troubles due to our sinful nature? **(The visual diagram in the Conclusion illustrates what happens in the human constitution through faith or a lack of faith, and the difference between human fate and divine destiny.)** In light of the previous statements, let me preface the answers by saying that "some" sins that are unintentional are mistakes. Now I know the latter statement sounds weak as a "lame" excuse and will be frowned upon by dogmatic thinkers based on their surface interpretation of translated Scripture. But a closer look at the diagram in the Conclusion can help to understand the point. Perhaps that's a problem bigger than sin itself which causes judgmental criticism of an imperfect weak life.

What's the point? The point is, just because you make mistakes, you are not a bad person or a sinner, and it doesn't always mean you caused your problems. **THE CHALLENGE!** And, just because you made mistakes and have problems doesn't mean you are not fit to serve God.

All of yesterday is in your past, and what matters most is today because you can't predict tomorrow. The wisdom of the Lord's parables (Metaphors that relate to practical life and Kingdom Concepts for living.) states that we should live in the moment, not in the past nor try to anticipate tomorrow. That's not approval of the philosophy of the Epicurians, or Hedonism which means living for pleasure in the moment. It means we can hope for tomorrow, but only God, in omniscience, knows tomorrow before it comes. So, trust God's plan and purpose for your life.

****

What was wrong with Job? He claimed innocence until God confronted him out of a whirlwind. (I believe it was a vision symbolized as the Eye of a Tornado.) God compared his existence to the universe and nature. It's a beautiful simile as it describes the Hand of God in creation. You can read it in Job 38:1-41. Up until that point, Job claimed innocence but God reproved him of being self-righteous. When we attempt to make ourselves right with God through the good things we do, we become self-righteous depending on what we do, not God. Job was wrong for that and God wanted him to see that clearly and to know God aside from his religious approach to God—**THE CHALLENGE.**

Don't get this wrong and continue reading for clarity, but God doesn't desire us to live a religiously structured life because it takes us away from living a normal life that God transforms. Why? Because religion is on the surface and conceals the real person. It can become a form of hypocrisy that blocks God from dealing with the heart. Also religion, that's void of a relationship with God shapes a person into a judgmental critic when their religious rules and regulations are not conformed to. Have you ever met mean-spirited religious people? Religion blocks compassion. God's not concerned with religious structure. God's not a God of religion.

The God of the sacred text of Scripture stands above religion, distinctly separate from other wanna-be small gods. The Lord is the God of the Universe and seeks to reach people in all religions. However, my point here is not about the Fatherhood of God and the Brotherhood of Man. Neither is it a joke or ridicule of religiously structured people. But some people (even Christians) need religious structure to live a better life. That's okay as long as the person serves God from the heart and not the head.

Some people may need a religiously structured life to keep them from going back to old addictions and bad habits. They become like the Wolfman during the full moon and need to be caged to prevent them from changing into monsters. Nevertheless, religiously structured lives can be so rigid that even God is prevented from getting through.

The purpose of one's spiritual journey is transformation into a Christ-like character. That cannot happen without the person opening their heart to the Lord and acknowledging that they are broken hurting people without God's help. Or, admitting that we have fallen short of God's revealed Will which is stated as "sin" in classic Christianity.

Always remember that God cannot reach a hypocrite because they are pretending to be someone they are not. Job saw that in the challenge, and in the end repented. *"I had heard of you by the hearing of the ear, but now my eye has seen you. Therefore I despise myself, and I repent in dust and ashes"* (Job 42:5-6).

Can you see it? Job, like many of us today had a head knowledge "about" God, but did not know God in a "personal" way from the heart. Like many of us today, he heard about God *superficially* through religious teachings and people; retained a head knowledge, but did not know God *intimately* (through a heart-to-heart personal relationship). That is until God opened his eyes. **To know the True and Living Lord, our eyes must be opened spiritually.**

The Greatest Challenge To Your Faith Isn't Any Person, Being, Or Thing. The Greatest Challenge To Your Faith Is You.

NEXT: *The Battle—Human Fate Ends Where Divine Destiny Begins*

CHAPTER 3

The Battle: Human Fate Ends Where Divine Destiny Begins!!!

Chapter Overview

The Creation Story, the Genesis Saga, and Creation Science are explored succinctly in light of Job's experiences and how those experiences parallel our lives. The great challenge to every Believer is how to overcome fate and embrace divine destiny. (Do we accept or reject the Lord when we are confronted by "conviction"?) The celestial scene in Job's life is compared to our problems that open our eyes to the forces behind our troubles. They are launched from cosmic/spiritual warfare. Here we look at the "possible" look of the spiritual realm through Scripture and extrabiblical quotes and examples. The key here is to overcome spiritual attacks on our lives not only by "Inviting" the Lord into our hearts, but we must invite the Lord into our "outer" circumstances and "Yield" to His presence in us.

Some scholars believe (and I do too) that there was a pre-Adamic earth before the Genesis Saga and Creation Story. You might ask, "Why would God create something so beautiful to become so troubled and destroy it in a worldwide flood in an instant?"

From the perspective of the Creation Story and Creation Science, the earth existed before time was introduced. Concerning geographical history and the earth's evolution, the earth is much older than time. This means inductively that the earth was created in eternity and is therefore eternal.

Some believe, and so do I that between Genesis 1:1 (which was a thesis statement of creation to come) and Genesis 1:2, God separates time from eternity and judges the pre-Adamic earth because of Lucifer's rebellion. Now I know that sounds like a Hollywood production, but *Truth* is stranger than fiction.

In my extensive inductive studies, Eden existed before God began the "re-creation" process of the earth in Genesis 1:2 which was destroyed upon the judgment of Lucifer and his rogue angels. According to Scripture references, I believe that it was occupied by Lucifer and the "Sons of God" (one-third of the hosts of heaven). They were God's creation for providence over human beings, created in the image of God.

It was a catastrophic/cosmic judgment that would reverberate like an atomic blast. It resulted in an empty world submerged in judgment by water. That is until God replenished it with the new creation, Adam and Eve, Sons and Daughters of the Morning. That title (Son of the Morning) was "actually" applied to Lucifer before his fall.

During eternity is where the showdown between God's Army and Satan's army meets in combat (Revelation 12:1-7) at the edge of the third dimension and the fourth dimension. It is also the place where Job's troubles began. So, let's begin looking at that place beginning with *the great challenge*.

—*The Great Challenge*—

As a believer, especially as a follower of the Lord, if you expect to reach your aspirations, be prepared for spiritual conflict. However, if you don't believe there is a spiritual realm in the universe, then spiritual battles don't matter. Fate will take its course.

In the saga of Job, Satan, the enemy of God and humanity appears at the threshold of heaven before God to challenge God's rule. Can you imagine that in the stellar heavens? Satan's challenge was twofold: First, Job saw his wealth as approval from God; Second, God protected him with wealth. That was Satan's argument and it appeared that way from the human perspective, but it wasn't God's way.

Please know and understand that Satan is not omniscient like God and doesn't know our thoughts like a "supposed" clairvoyant or invades our thoughts through telepathy. But he does know our history and draws from our history to challenge God and our lives. And like a bully, he will pick on your weaknesses. So don't be anxious about how you live, but be careful because how you live can be used against you! That's always the backdrop behind our trials and temptations; the confusion of where is this trouble coming from and why. Is God behind our trials or is it the devil?

Satan's accusation against Job came from his knowledge of Job's history. Somewhere along the line, he detected that Job's faith was wrapped up in his wealth. The source will determine your action but it begins with discernment.

Cosmic/Spiritual Warfare

When we talk about God using (working through) people or even devils using people, what we are talking about more than anything is spiritual warfare behind the scenes.

The paranormal, supernatural, and psychic phenomena can lead to opening a portal to the dark arts (spell casting) if dabbled in, and with the right mix of drugs can induce hallucinations of an alternate reality (Revelation 22:15). (Be careful with hypnotist, especially if you drink something before being hypnotized.) Although some of the things mentioned can be correlated with Scripture (imitation is the most sincere form of flattery) it is still an alternate reality. So, I'll begin this section by transitioning into a collaborative description of the spiritual realm by using some quotes and analogies to distinguish the difference.

To the chagrin of some, I just mentioned "spell casting" and most people are skeptical about such things as superstitions, folklore, or old wives' tales. However, Scripture mentions those things as real. That is to those who believe it is real. Remember magic takes place in the mind and if you do not believe it, it will not have an effect on your mind.

Scripture teaches that an idol (in and of itself) is nothing and that those who make offerings to idols are "actually" worshipping demons that lurk behind the idols (1 Corinthians 8).

However, to make it seem real, magic seeks to harness technology which is the source of the illusions of the mind, and the laws of nature through rituals and conjuring. They also use herbs and plants as a source of health, wealth, and curses.

[There are three Scriptural insights to consider when discerning whether magic is real. But first, get the fantasies and fabrications of Hollywood productions out of your mind. Second, the Scripture states that an idol is nothing except for the person who believes it is real. Third, Scripture states that *"The arrival of the lawless one will be by Satan's working with all kinds of miracles and signs and false wonders"* **(2 Thessalonians 9:8). What's the point? Note, "false" wonders are translated as "lying" wonders in the KJV. The point is that devils fabricate illusions to deceive people into believing the BIG LIE spawned by Satan (John 8:44). A lie isn't real and cannot harm or hurt you unless you believe it.**

However, Job's disasters initiated by Satan were real only because God permitted it. So, remember that if we are significant to God's calling, we become a threat to the devil and our lifestyle becomes his target of attack that results in real things happening. So, adjust your lifestyle!]

Nonetheless, the above is a paradox in that the things mentioned can also be used for good, minus illusions and delusions. So, discernment is the key to distinguishing the difference which is why Scripture admonishes Believers to condemn the practices of the dark arts. Whether you believe it or not, God gives us a prescription to protect us from such evil. The prescription is simply faith in the Living Lord. So, allow me to drift a bit from the theme then come back and substantiate the point about Job's spiritual attack and consequently what can happen to us amid our troubles.

In most cases, when I speak of the source of some trouble and trauma, I'm pointing to a higher plane of conflict that targets believers and those seeking God-Truth. They are under spiritual attack because of their faith and practice. The pivotal question is, do we believe in a spiritual conflict that seeks to prevent our progress in the "things of the Lord."

The Celestial Scene

Corresponding passages of **Scripture**, **Creation Science**, and **Astronomy** can be correlated, and agree that there are *three dimensions* to our world and universe. I'll begin with *the third dimension*, our physical world. We don't know much about our oceans and seas which constitute the first and second dimensions.

The third dimension is our atmospheric heaven stretched out in "spheres" that travel beyond the clouds into the troposphere, stratosphere, mesosphere,

thermosphere, and exosphere-ionosphere. After that, we are in outer space (the stellar heavens) where gravity and oxygen decrease. **Outer space or the Astral Plane constitutes the fourth dimension.**

Try to create a picture of this in your mind and imagine these quotes from The Pleiades (In Greek mythology, they were the seven daughters of the Titan Atlas and the Oceanid Pleione: Maia, Electra, Taygete, Celaeno, Alcyone, Sterope, and Merope. They all had children by gods except Merope, who married Sisyphus.) **The Pleiades eventually identified a star constellation and these thoughts are from the star constellation or what they point out as the spiritual realm.**

Mythology or Astrology is indirectly forbidden in Scripture, and neither do I base my statements and points on those spiritualist distinctives. But mythology is the human imagination and philosophy about gods, constellations, elements of the earth, and how gods govern the universe. It can also be seen as magic. These are not my views, but I do think it's interesting to note any correlation between what is recorded in Scripture and what you believe will give meaning to your faith. (Eliminate the Negative and Accentuate the Positive) In some ways, it looks at human beings as little gods of their created worlds and to me, that's New Age philosophies because they combine spiritualism with science and technology. But they make the point in the stretch of their imagination. Now some thoughts about those realms from the Pleiades:

["The Third Dimension-Physical Reality of the Conscious Being. The Third Dimension is where energy converges into a dark, dense pool of matter... The Universe allows the illusion of Free-Will on the Third and Fourth Dimensions which gives us the experience of acting like saints or

*demons or somewhere in between . . . by choice."
"Beings believing that the Third is the only Dimension suffer from the illusion of separation from their Spirit. The physical senses cannot detect Spirit which is beyond form . . . If we are not One with Spirit then we cannot be at one with others. This Dimension of Thought has the ability to interpenetrate all of life, like a sort of etheric river of water. It is not confined to the brain, which actually acts more like a kind of telephone switching station to all the thoughts that pass through it . . . Our ability to experience beauty while in such density, shows that we live in a loving Universe . . . (The etheric body can be characterised as the life force also present in the plant kingdom. It maintains the physical body's form until death. At that time, it separates from the physical body and the physical reverts to natural disintegration") . . . Humans possess a body made up of the material of the Physical Plane world . . . a body containing chemicals in liquid, solid and gaseous states. This body is interpenetrated by another body, which is its counterpart, known as the Etheric Body. It constitutes a fine web through which the Electromagnetic Life-forces are fed into the physical body from the outer Universe."
(https://www.bibliotecapleyades.net/ciencia/ciencia_dimensionshyperdimensions.htm#contents)]*

From these quotes, I think you will be able to draw the line between spirituality and spiritualism. It is a fine line of discernment.

The quotes above are from spiritualists who see spiritual life and spiritual beings as the highest form of life in the universe. As you continue to read, you will see that spiritualism imitates spirituality (The journey of those who follow the Lord.) and can confuse the path that one chooses to follow. You will also see a semblance of what Scripture refers to as eternal life or immortality. But remember, spiritualists try to create an alternative way to God that can lead to spiritual conflict resulting in trials and temptations.

So, the battle between God's angels (Hebrews 1:14 calls angels "ministering spirits sent to serve those who will inherit salvation.") and Satan's fallen angels (Demons), one-third of the hosts of heaven takes place between these two realms.

I believe that the fourth dimension is the headquarters of demonic activity today that first targets *governments* then *religions*, then *society* (Ephesians 6:10-12). I also believe that UFOs and Aliens occupy the third and fourth dimensions and are fallen angels in disguise to deceive and lead humanity astray. I also believe that mythological gods are also demons transforming their image (shape-shifters). **The conversation between God and Satan in Job 1-2 takes place in this realm.** This is also the place where charges are brought against all God's servants. **Now the fifth dimension.**

First, here's an editorial thought: Just in case angels violated their free will and attacked humanity; suppose God created one-third of the innumerable angels as guardians in the pre-Adamic earth for divine providence for humans. (Sounds like "Star Wars," right.) Then suppose Lucifer was given charge of the angels (Sons of God) to watch over humans (Whom Christ referred to as guardian angels.). But suppose humans "seemed" to be more important than the angels and occupied a higher plane than angels because they were created in the image of God. Given the tenets of free will, do you think Lucifer could have become jealous and envious of their privilege and prestige with God and decided to challenge God's judgment? *"Of what importance is the human race, that you should notice them? Of what importance is mankind, that you should pay attention to them? You made them a little less than the heavenly beings. You crowned mankind with honor and majesty. You appoint them to rule over your creation; you have placed everything under their authority"* (Psalms 8:4-6).

(During eternity, when Lucifer became corrupted with INORDINATE pride, comparable to extreme narcissism today, his vast knowledge of the universe, along with his beauty arrayed in precious gems, he lied to the Sons of God—one-third of the host of heaven—to form a spiritual coup against God.

[The idea behind the nature of "iniquity" comes from Satan's insurrection against God. It means more than sin. It means willfully going against the revealed Will of God called "Unbelief" by the Lord that cannot be forgiven. Not that God will not forgive. But rather, God can not forgive because the person shuts their heart from God and refuses to repent of their free will. Thus it means to rebel against God's rule. It's all consistent with free will.]

The fourth dimension is also the realm of MAGIC and magic is about dabbling in the realm of the supernatural/paranormal. So let me reiterate: Magic can open destructive portals into the dark arts. So, although I do not support or encourage people to consult these sources for direction and guidance in life, it's good to know these things to discern truth from error. Now the fifth dimension.

> *["**The Fifth Dimension-Heaven** ... The Plane of Light. For most religions, the Fifth Dimension is the highest realms a Soul can reach. Spiritually, starting from the beginning, it is the last stop downward on the dimensional ladder before we enter the realms of limitation. We incarnate here as androgynous stellar beings. Since we live on Stars we have luminous Light Bodies. These eternal forms do not need for pain, the warning signals that physical bodies provide. Therefore there is no physical suffering. Neither do we suffer from any form of separation because we constantly experience the Oneness of Mother/Father Creator.* **(Note: Use your imagination here and I think it will be easy to see that spiritualists see the spiritual life as the highest form of life that is immortal. So why is it so hard for people to believe in the gift of eternal life offered by the Lord of Glory? Now let's continue with the Pleiades quotes.)**
>
> *We base our actions entirely on Love, never fear. This is because fear does not exist at this level. We are unstoppable and living Miraculous lives. Immortality is an experiential given. Many times in a Near Death Experience, a person will travel thru a long tunnel. The tunnel traverses the darkness (the Fourth Dimension) and ends in a bright opening of Golden or White Light (the Fifth Dimension). This is the Birth Canal of the Soul and the doorway to Heaven.*
>
> *We travel by application of Divine Will. We need not die to have this experience. The shortest distance between two points is not a straight line or curved*

line. In the Fifth Dimension, one simply duplicates herself to her destination(s). We travel by moving through the doorway at the center of the star. We do not fly as this movement is similar to teleportation. Flying is only a viable means of transportation on the Third and Fourth Dimensions.

In many Ascension stories, the Earth transforms... along with her inhabitants into her fifth-dimensional Light Body. This is when Gaia physically shifts from a dense, material body to one of Light... A Star. The present Earth changes and Ancient prophecies are guides to this probable future. However, the Fifth Dimensional Manifestation of a star is neither hot nor fiery... It is soft. This is known as THE MIRACULOUS WORLD..."
(https://www.bibliotecapleyades.net/ciencia/ciencia_dimensionshyperdimensions.htm#contents)]

Although the editorial above sounds very eclectic and convoluted, my point is to show just that. God's plans and purpose are not complicated. They are simple enough for a child to understand when it is explained properly. So, if we can believe the extremely bizarre things presented by Spiritualists and other outlandish out-of-space things by other conspiracy theorists, why can't we believe that the Lord was incarnated, died, rose, and ascended back to glory? **I hope you "get" the point, that there is a spiritual realm in our universe where life challenges originate that can make us or break us. Either way, if we follow God's pre-ordained plan, our years to come will be brighter and better.**

CONFRONTED

My encounter with the Lord that transformed my life began in 1974. I was at my wit's end concerning the hope of my future. I ended up in constant trouble with the law because of a downward spiral in my lifestyle. It got so bad that I was tempted to cross the line and start selling drugs and enter the crime scene. **(That's when "my" human fate clashed with divine destiny. I was faced with a decision to change my course of life after being "confronted" by the presence of the Lord in my conscience.)** At the point where I was about to give up and give in to the demands of a lifestyle gone bad, the Lord stepped in through faith and my fate (of a life going down fast) changed to the divine destiny of a life progressing upward.

When something is going wrong in life and headed in the wrong direction, something must happen (circumstantially) or someone must confront the one headed in the wrong direction. The hard part is that confrontation is like accountability. Therefore few people see it for what it's worth. Few people like being confronted because it's like an interrogation. Whether by a person or circumstance, we are confronted when we are faced with a crisis that necessitates an important decision. The most important decision of my life was to accept the Lord as my Personal Savior.

Before retirement, I was seen as a confrontational pastor, but I saw it as strong leadership. Confrontation was the first phase of my process for ethnic and cultural reconciliation as I worked with both white and black churches and leadership development. The question is, do we "really" desire to grow spiritually and become the best person that God has made us to be? If the answer is yes, then confrontation is the first prescription for healing and wholeness.

My purpose for confrontation was drawn from the pages of Scripture that led me to a transformed life. If you will, a heart transplant. That is, a change in the heart (The Soul or Inner Person) that affects the outer person. It wasn't for the sake of an argument. Rather, it was for identifying a problem of the past that required assessment to develop a plan for better relationships. (That becomes a topic of Wounded Healers.) So, let me say here for the sake of "naysayers" who deny dialoguing the past as a means of correcting the present and future and insist on saying, "Get over it." Getting over it is easier said than done when the cycle of the past continues.

I do not believe that we can repeat history. Astronomically speaking, for history to repeat itself is like the earth reversing its rotation on its axis and the person taking a quantum leap into the past. IMPOSSIBLE!

We can't change the past but we can correct the present by assessing problems of the past that plague us today. Nonetheless, history can catch up to us if we have not dealt with the critical problems of the past. According to the sacred text, some past problems can follow us or go before us. *"The sins of some people are obvious, going before them into judgment, but for others, they show up later* (1 Timothy 5:24). It means that we will not get away with doing evil things just because we are not judged now. But they will follow us into eternity.

Remember, Satan knows our history (past) and influences a replay of the mistakes and the worst things that happened in our past. That causes emotional grief and unnecessary guilt and shame. Remember, Satan is not omniscient like God but he knows our history from day one. So, he brings up the negative and toxic things from our past to hinder and handicap our progression with the Lord by pointing out the guilt and shame of our past. This is especially true when we are engaged in ministry to people who committed similar acts.

When a believer is confronted either by a loving caring individual or is under conviction in the heart based on unwise circumstances; God is admonishing the person to change the course of their direction that will bring them into a closer relationship with the Lord. Therefore, whether by a professional therapist or a therapeutic Word from Scripture from a person who loves the Lord; that kind of confrontation is the first step toward treatment for unresolved problems. **Job was confronted by the Almighty from within the whirlwind (tornado) and the confrontation "pricked" his heart and he repented.**

****

With every life test comes a temptation, or behind every test from God is a temptation from the devil. The temptation can lure you into taking the shortcut or the easy way out, which can be the wrong way by avoiding any form of confrontation because it hurts your feelings. A test from God will take you along a route that faces and confronts the problem and your feelings, which can be the right way but hurts. Job chose to take the test and passed in the end. The devil vehemently wants us to fail the test by yielding to the temptation to take the easy way out. God desires us to pass the test, so we don't have to take it again. The issue of being tested is a matter of our faith.

In my faith perspective, divine destiny begins at the point of acknowledging Yeshua (Jesus) as Lord and is followed up with verbal acknowledgment from the heart. From that point onward our lives are no longer governed by the course of the fickled finger of fate referred to as "the flesh" in Scripture, but by divine plan for our present and future. The past is dead and has no "say so" regarding our present and future. But, the problems we encountered in the past can still haunt us if we revert to our old ways, and return with a vengeance. Either way, walking in the newness of life or resorting back to our old ways, we will still have hurt, pain, wounds, and bruises in need of **treatment**.

****

Job's confrontation was twofold. It began with a confrontation between Satan and the Lord in the heavenlies then came down in the form of disasters and escalated between Job and his "so-called" friends. And, if we are disciples of the Lord, following the ways of the Lord, our conflicts, likewise begin with an encounter of heavenly hosts then we are faced with the natural consequences that require spiritual battle. However, the spiritual battle isn't between us and the devil. We would lose that battle every time if not for the Lord intervening on our behalf. It wouldn't even be a battle because human beings are not subject to fighting spiritual beings. Scripture says, "We Wrestle Not With Flesh And Blood" (Ephesians 6:12), meaning our fight is not against a person or persons. But, it is spiritual forces that influence people that must be combatted and we are not equipped for that battle. That battle is the Lord's which is why the armor of God is important (Ephesians 6).

To fight in that battle is like a tag-team wrestling match. When confronted by negativity and toxic resistance, spiritually speaking, we must step out of the ring and "INVITE" the Lord to fight that battle for us. Nevertheless, the battle can cause injuries, and leave bruises and scars from our initial encounters.

If the influence of your problems came from the spiritual realm then the battle will be in the spiritual realm too. But you will not be involved. It will be between Satan's fallen angels and God's anointed angels who stand guard over your life. **Our responsibility in spiritual battles is to pray the prayer of importunity (Luke 18) and YIELD to the Lord.**

—*YIELDING*—

The main challenge to your faith is the conflict between your inner divinity and outer humanity called, "flesh and Spirit." Whichever one wins, will determine whether you achieve your vision, purpose, and plans, and defeat your spiritual enemies.

"But I say, live by the Spirit and you will not carry out the desires of the flesh. For the flesh has desires that are opposed to the Spirit, and the Spirit has desires that are opposed to the flesh, for these are in opposition to each other, so that you cannot do what you want" (Galatians 5:16-17).

As I close this chapter, note the conflict from the Scripture above is between flesh and Spirit (referred to as soul and body on the diagram in the Conclusion), and remember, the human spirit is the dwelling place of God's Spirit.

We can see from various Scriptures "yielding" is about giving way to God's revealed Will in us. So, what I am saying is that "divine intervention" is not about God dropping out of heaven and like a "bull in a china closet" rampaging our circumstances and people. Divine intervention is about a believer or multiple believers "inviting" God into their circumstances by opening their hearts for the Lord to have His way.

The results of multiple believers "yielding" to God in prayer and experiencing divine intervention are taken from the Book of Acts (Acts 12:3–19).

Peter is falsely imprisoned because he declared the Gospel. Not the gospel of denominationalism or doctrine related to local churches because those views vary and didn't exist at that time. But the Gospel of the Kingdom of God is recorded in Matthew 24:14. The religious community saw what he preached as heresy. However, before the gathering of believers could finish their prayer, an angel of the Lord had released peter from prison and he made his way to where they were praying, and showed up at the door while they were still praying. You can imagine their surprise, but that's intervention in our circumstances. The difference today is we don't see what happens in the spiritual realm that changes our circumstances. **Here's a closing example of what I mean:**

When you are driving along a stretch of road and come to a cross-section, you will either come to a traffic light, stop sign, yield sign, or no sign at all. But even if there is no sign, it's best to slow down, and look both ways, or you could get into an accident. ***That's what it means to slow down and decide on your direction.*** *You have the power of choice to obey the traffic light if it's green to go or red to stop. If you run the red light, you stand the chance of getting a ticket, or worse, getting into an accident and dying. That's the way it is when we ignore the signs within us that we are violating the moral law and problems get worse. Then there is the stop sign. If you run a stop sign the same thing can happen. Then there is the yield sign where I draw my point. The yield sign means that when you come to the intersection, you must slow down, look both ways, and proceed with caution.*

That's the point of healing from our traumas and problems. We must slow down and decide if we will continue straight ahead or turn right or left. When contemplating our problems, if we continue straight ahead, we are still going in the same direction that got us in trouble. We must yield (weigh our decision) and turn right or left.

Yielding is essentially "INVITING" the Lord into the circumstances of our personal lives. Hear this clearly and carefully because when it comes to our "personal" relationship with the Lord, we normally don't think this way. Nonetheless, it's not enough to "just" invite the Lord into our hearts. That's the beginning . . . Because the Lord works through free

will, the Lord will not intervene in our troubling circumstances without our invitation to give us new direction and chase away people who trouble us. THAT AUTHORIZES OUR VICTORY!

NEXT: *Progressing Toward Healing: Spiritual CPR*

CHAPTER 4

Progressing Toward Healing: Spiritual CPR

Here we will identify the roadblocks to our progress and examine the crisis in our lives as a turning point to elevate our thinking (Faith Assent). It means that a crisis is a turning point and we must choose wisely our direction. The point is, to choose the right direction during a crisis we must practice the essentials of our faith: confession (between us and the Lord initially) repentance, forgiveness, and renouncing in some cases. The acronym CPR is used as a tool to resuscitate one's spiritual life. PACE is used as an acronym that spells out "Peace At Christ's Expense." Peace becomes a navigation device that helps us to see our way out of a foggy situation. Finally, we review the restoration process of Job when he received twice as much as he had before when he repented of his claim to innocence and forgave his friends.

For the sake of our mental and emotional health, it is important to find your purpose in life. Your purpose in life can give meaning to the things that you go through, especially when your objective in life is to help others. That is, your experiences in life are about your personal growth and development that impresses others. So, look at all you go through as a means of witnessing to others that they can make it through their crisis. Or, you can look at it this way:

We don't know what's ahead of us in the next second. That's how fragile life is. Nevertheless, God does. To get through our problems we must believe that we will overcome the difficulties that we face.

In "some" situations, God "may" permit something bad to happen in the present but God doesn't cause it to happen because that would violate free will. So, when something bad happens, God "may" allow it to prevent something worse from happening later. For example:

> *It had snowed heavily for several days in a New England town. The snow blanketed the roofs of the houses not in inches but several feet of snow. During that time of emergency, a thief broke into one of the homes while the family was asleep. By accident, he found his way into the baby's room while the infant slept. He began plundering for something to steal and accidentally knocked over a lamp that shattered on the floor. The sound woke the baby up and he let out a loud cry. Down the hall from the infant room, the mother instinctively heard the baby's cry, jumped out of her bed, sprinted down the hall, opened the door and saw the thief, went and scooped the baby up out of its crib, and ran back out the door. When she slammed the door behind her and reached safety she heard a crashing sound coming from the baby's room. The roof caved in under the weight of the snow, unfortunately crushing the thief. All the mother could say was, "Thank God for the thief."*

Note that God permits, but it is the free will choice of the person regarding what they do. God doesn't "make" them do what they do. So, it becomes our responsibility to discern what God is doing. Unfortunately, within some faith perspectives, God is seen like some kind of Genie in a lamp that if rubbed in the right place we will get our wishes granted. That only happens in fairy tales.

—*The Roadblocks*—

Concerning our goals and objectives in life, *"Shoot for the Moon. Even if you miss, you'll land among the stars"* (Norman Vincent Peale). That quote should be the aim of life to its fullest. Nevertheless, before we can say that in good conscience, we must address the roadblocks and the biggest roadblock is answering the elusive pervading question, "Why do bad things happen to good people?" For that matter, "Why do good things happen to bad people."

Life, at times, seems to be so unfair to us. When we are doing our best, why do things turn out not-so-good? Well, recovery is a process of restoring losses and takes time. I know many of you reading this have been there. It is "actually" a journey towards a better life. But, to get there is a refining process through good and bad that shapes a well-rounded fulfilled life. That's the aim of those seeking "to live their best life now." Here's a formula: Spiritual CPR.

Normally, we refer to the natural procedure CPR as the acronym for the medical terminology of Cardiac Pulmonary Resuscitation: A method of reviving arrested heart conditions. Just as a shortage of blood flow to our hearts due to hardened arteries can result in heart attacks, thus requiring CPR, there are times when our faith and spiritual arteries are hardened because of difficulties, frustration, and disappointment and we lose sight of our direction. That too lessens the life-giving flow of faith that can restore the lack of vision in our spiritual hearts and requires a form of resuscitation. The difference is CPR here stands for understanding the **Crisis**; **Pace**; and **Restoration which are challenges to our Faith**.

THE CRISIS

A crisis is a *turning point* that is usually imposed on one's life at unsuspecting times, leaving us bewildered. We all have crises that we knowingly or unknowingly will encounter. That's life! A crisis comes with some form of trouble that becomes a problem that we must figure out like a puzzle. The dilemma for many is finding the answer and solution.

Many of the problems and troubles we face are out of our control, but the solution is within reach. As a turning point, a crisis requires a decision regarding the direction to take. It's like coming to a fork in the road. Do we go right or left? Or, can we just pave our "own" way and go straight ahead? In the simplicity of a spiritually guided life, our faith perspective should provide an answer.

God, in omniscient wisdom (all-knowing), has an answer but are we willing to choose God's way when we are not sure because, humanly speaking, it doesn't seem like the best way? That's where faith comes in and we shouldn't become pessimistic about faith because all of life requires some level of faith. Faith encompasses all of our decisions in life whether we can see the results or are oblivious to the results. Every day when we wake up, we must make a faith decision to get up and go about our routines. Then it starts all over the next day. Sometimes it may feel like we are in a "time loop," experiencing "Groundhog Day" or some sort of Deja Vu. We've all felt it from time to time.

Faith is believing against all odds and never giving up on one's dreams for a better life. "Hoping against Hope" means that we have doubts but we still hope. Strong believers still hope when it seems hopeless, like Abraham, the Father of the Faithful. Faith and hope never come without doubt, but faith presses against doubt. **In pragmatic terms, it means that we will have mixed emotions about our direction that we must cast aside.** But harken, given the complexities of life, there will be challenges that stand in the way of reaching that better life.

Faith, like financial investment, requires taking a chance with the possibilities. We don't think at the moment this way, but when we do think about it, many of life's decisions are a gamble. That's risky and most people aren't willing to take a risk, especially with their money. That brings us to a pertinent point about faith and money. Let's do some situational analysis of Job's predicament that will flesh out in the pages to come. **His wealth seems to be at the core of his crisis!**

It matters not whether we do not believe in God or the devil because it doesn't change the reality of the verifiable existence of good and evil in the world. Evil is described as destructive and good is constructive. When good things happen, people improve and rejoice. When bad things happen, people cower in the corner of life, either out of anger or hate. Or, they will sink into fear and depression.

The question of faith is, is there an entity behind good and evil, and if so, can they be identified? That is, can the influences of people be identified as good or evil, and the answer is an emphatic yes because there are human demagogues. Demagogues become dictators and dictators "attempt" to usurp the place of God.

****

As difficult as the previous statement may sound, and the dread of the pain we must endure during a crisis in our human experience, the outcome far outweighs the trial. **(We will explore how God uses crises to direct our lives and examine the purpose of trauma and**

trouble.) Is that even possible, to get to the bottom of our problems? I don't think so because the depth of our problems (as you will see) stretches to heaven. We need God's perspective and the perspectives of others (negative and positive) to align with the best solution. So, get yourself a good prayer partner. ("Two heads are better than One.") No one sees the same problem identically. So the answer to the question is no we can't get to the bottom of every problem because the root of all problems goes back to the first humans and are complex problems with different acts and outcomes. But we can find a solution to "any" problem in the Lord if we are willing to rely upon Him for answers.

The associated problem with finding a solution is being problem-fixated instead of solution-oriented. Of course, to fix a problem we must know the causes and those causes will reveal themselves as we progress toward a solution. There is an array of problems that every human being will face, but the difference will be how we **pace** ourselves through the difficulties. They won't magically go away but we will be enabled to get through them and move on from them.

THE PACE

How you manage your crisis and trouble can be affected by the pace you set for your life. That is, the timeline for hopefully achieving your goals. For example, where do you "believe" you will be in 3-5 years? We'll talk more about that later but for now, let me put it in my faith perspective, and you can go ahead and put it in your faith perspective too.

The analysis of pace in one's life begins by knowing where you've come from and how you got started. It's important and therapeutic to write our memories and recap significant events as far back as we can remember.

Although some are late bloomers, human nature can be defined in terms of chronological development from infancy, through toddlerhood, childhood, adolescence, young adulthood, adulthood, midlife, and old age.

Each stage of human development is about maturing as a responsible adult. One can not achieve spiritual maturity without reaching natural maturity. Natural development is a precursor of spiritual growth. **This is why I state that chronological development runs parallel with spiritual maturity.** For example, you can't take a 30-year-old man and expect him to be spiritually mature and responsible when he hasn't found his identity as a teenager and young adult.

At each critical stage of development, the identity of the person should be established, especially during puberty, otherwise, they can continue in life experiencing an identity crisis and immaturity. Thus, even the Lord went through a rite of passage at 12 years old and was allowed to interact with adults in the Temple addressing leading questions about faith and religion.

Due to my extensive education process, I tend to use mnemonic devices in the form of acronyms to remember important things. So PACE in that light is "Peace At Christ's Expense." The reason is that we need peace of mind or a clear head when it comes to making decisions. Problems, like a natural fog, make it difficult to see your way out.

Human logic can become irrational when faced with the complexity of problems and impulsively (on the spur of the moment) make a wrong decision. Emotionally speaking, we must wait until the smoke clears to correctly see the options. So think of peace like a navigation device that can guide you out of a foggy situation. Does your faith perspective give you peace of mind?

The most difficult aspect of our troubles is the waiting period to see what will happen next. During that phase we must wait, like a person on trial, waiting for the verdict from the jury. If you have ever been in court for a misdemeanor or something more serious, you know what I mean. You become filled with anxiety concerning the verdict, and then you have to endure the pain of the outcome of the trial, especially if you are found guilty. But the "good news" of faith in the Lord of Glory is we are not on trial when we go through trials. I know it's an oxymoron, but, in my "personal" faith perspective, God through the atoning work of the Lord has not "merely" acquitted me of past shortcomings, mistakes, and errors of judgment as past sins, by casting them in the metaphorical "sea of forgetfulness," God has deleted them. (Here's something unfathomable: They no longer exist in the Mind of God.) It means in the infinite mind of God, God no longer remembers our sins and does not call them up because God's purity (referred to as holiness) cannot look upon that which is sin. ("He's of holier eyes . . ."—Habakkuk 1:13).

God sees every believer in Christ, our Lord as a new creation; if you will, a new species. It is the job of the "Accuser of the brethren" to bring up past sins, so know where condemnation comes from. God "convicts" but doesn't condemn. Thus, I've been set free from past failures, and declared righteous, as though I never committed any wrong. I have a clean slate to work with every day. That's called "justification" in the plan of redemption: God pardons us and gives us a fresh start every day. **My focus is not on my past errors (sins) but on my current opportunity (the freedom of salvation) to get better.** *"Now the Lord is the Spirit,* *and where the Spirit of the Lord is present, there is freedom"* (2 Corinthians 3:17).

Life is like a marathon and not like a sprint race competing against "The Joneses" to see who can come in first with their wealth and material possessions. Most people who participate in a marathon do so, not to try to come in first, but for the joy of finishing the race. In the Lord, it's not how you start, but how you finish. In God's Eyes, we want to finish on top of our game because that perspective brings rewards for the task before you when you need it the most.

To finish a marathon race, each runner must know their level of energy and strength, measured strides, and when they need to slow the pace and pick up the pace. Two things should never happen when nearing the finish line: Don't look to the side or back at your competition or past failures or you might trip up or lose ground, and save some energy for the sprint at the end. That is, the task it will take to transition you to a higher level of living. ***Breakthrough!***

When we are faced with a crisis or problem, we ask ourselves a multitude of questions that riddle our conscience: How can I get through this mess I'm in? Is it all worth it? Can I maintain my sanity and sense of composure? Will I fall apart and have an emotional or nervous breakdown? Most importantly, can I hold on to my hope? My answer is yes to it all if we can pace ourselves.

Pacing yourself will enable you to experience what I call *renewal* **and** *revival.* **Each day can be a new beginning in your life. I call it Restoration.**

THE RESTORATION

According to the sacred text, God desires to restore our lives by putting us back together according to God's divine design. *"Acknowledge him in all your ways, and he will make your paths straight. Do not be wise in your own estimation; fear the Lord and turn away from evil.* **This will bring healing to your body, and refreshment to your inner self**" (Proverbs 3:6-8).

"*Humpty Dumpty sat on a wall. Humpty Dumpty had a great fall. All the king's horses and all the king's men, couldn't put Humpty Dumpty together again.*" The origin of this four-line poem is not clear. Humpty Dumpty was a giant egg, making him fragile. I think we can assume Humpty Dumpty was the king with wealth and power. His fall could mean his defeat by a rival king and that he lacks the power to be put back together by his men. His source of help failed him. What do we do when those around us and our faith perspective fail us? Do we turn against the people and lose faith in our God, or do we tap into the reality of life that says, "This too will pass," repent and forgive and move on?

What a tragic nursery rhyme, to say the least for children! Can you imagine a huge hollow egg-like character, broken into tiny pieces, lying scattered along the ground? Yet, it could be a tragic picture of any of us at any time. Somewhere in life, we can have a "great fall" and experience brokenness or even homelessness because our emotions were damaged and we spin our wheels trying to put ourselves back together again. The problem is we try to put ourselves back together in the energy of our depleted strength, without any help from God. It only leads to rationalization and justification of what happened and animosity for those who judged us.

Due to human frailty and faults, more times than not, people will fail us which can cause feelings of brokenness. Then we try different means of putting ourselves back together, which become coping mechanisms. It could be drugs, alcohol, sex, gluttony, gambling, greed for wealth by any means, etc. Although we may not want to admit it, these things become a person's drug of choice. But sooner or later that will fail too and compound our problems with more emptiness.

I don't know the circumstances and situations that people reading this have faced in their journey through life. But I do know what can happen when people stand on the outside looking in and misjudge what they see on the inside, or the consequences of what happened and misunderstand the person and their situation. Sometimes those misunderstandings can lead to betrayal and people who come into the misunderstood person's life, can betray them, turn their backs on them, and walk out of their lives with misconstrued information about them that turns into gossip and rumors. That hurts deeply like betrayal that I call "the Judas Effect." It lends to brokenness and we can feel like Humpty Dumpty: defeated in life.

NEXT: *What's Ailing You: Healing from Pain?!*

CHAPTER 5

What's Ailing You: Healing from Pain?!

Chapter Overview

Pain is the result of humanity's fall and a sign of our mortal frailty and weakness and can be experienced physically, mentally, emotionally, and spiritually. Pain reminds us that we are dying to live. But the emphasis is not on dying but on living! We look at Job and how we can push our way through the pain of losses, even death. But it becomes a matter of releasing our faith. And releasing our faith is a matter of giving in to the Will of God prescribed by the Word of the Lord. The healing factor becomes the virtue of the Lord in us that can be released. Will it heal? That depends, but it will help to cope. We will examine how stress can overwhelm us, how circumstances and people can crush us, and how it begins with fear. Then we will go through the major types of trauma and trouble that can impact our lives negatively. We end the chapter with a look at spiritual cleansing from trauma and trouble like taking a shower under the flow of God's Spirit.

The life of a disciple of the Lord is not a mirror reflection of a perfect world, heaven. Although heaven is blissful perfection, we are not there yet. We are imperfect people, living in an imperfect world. In terms of our imperfect human nature, we face two arenas of trouble: the natural side of life and the spiritual side of life. To understand the natural, we must get insight into the spiritual. But, to gain spiritual insight, we must penetrate the pain associated with spiritual growth.

****

Pain reminds us that we are dying. But as believers, we must keep in mind that the Lord came to bring us life, and life more abundantly. So, as we understand the nature of God's presence in us we can experience God's lifegiving flow of spiritual healing from within us through the indwelling of the Spirit. Listen, God is within us so why can't we tap into the virtuous provisions that God has promised?

God's remedial presence in us can affect our mental, emotional, and physical condition if we can release our faith. (Releasing our faith is a matter of giving in to the Will of God prescribed by the Word of the Lord. Romans 10:17, *"So then faith comes by hearing, and hearing by the word of God."*)

"A cheerful heart brings good healing, but a crushed spirit dries up the bones" (Proverbs 17:22). When God's virtue within us is released from our human spirit we can experience healing. (During the Lord's public ministry, virtue went out from Him and healed the recipients.)

God's source of healing starts by mending broken hearts. (All forms of broken hearts begin with a broken relationship.) But our brokenness can become the beginning of healing for ourselves and others. Wounds can produce empathy in us to be considerate and compassionate about others who have experienced the same problems.

I feel the looming pain for people who seemingly want a picture-perfect life. They will be the ones who are disappointed the most and crushed by people and circumstances when things go wrong.

If older people (back in the day) had an idea or an intuitive feeling that something was wrong with a person, they would ask, "What's ailing you?" They somehow could see our pain because our pain was that obvious. The truth is, things got better if we took heed to what they were saying. The Lord has healing for what ails us if we take heed.

****

An ailment is something or someone who causes you chronic pain or discomfort as a threat to your life. Or, it can give you an eerie sense that something bad is about to happen. Let's take a look at the pain and discomfort of trauma and trouble extracted from the life of Job to be applied to common everyday experiences.

Can you imagine the initial shock to Job's system when he suddenly heard the disastrous news? Bad news was on the heel of bad news: His oxen and donkeys were stolen by the marauding Sabeans (Job 2:13-15) and all his herdsmen were killed, except the messenger of bad news. Before he could finish his story, another messenger came on the tail-end of the first messenger's story and said an electrical storm destroyed all the sheep and the sheepherders (Job 2:16). If that wasn't enough, before that bearer of bad news could finish his story, the other bearer of bad news rushed in and said, the Chaldeans raided the camels and killed the servants (Job 2:17). But it wasn't over yet. Another messenger came with the worst news that a man would want to hear. All of his children lost their lives in a hurricane that popped up from the wilderness (Job 2:18-19).

Based on the comparison of Scripture, Job's lucrative business was breeding and raising livestock (animals for home and profit) and he was very successful at it according to Satan himself. But he went from Great Wealth to Poverty Instantly!

Our sense of being Stressed, Overwhelmed, and Crushed by Circumstances and People begins with Fear.

Fear is one of the arsenal weapons that Satan uses to attack God's people who are the greatest threats to him and his schemes. Consequently, Satan attacks the major areas of our lives to trip us up along our mission journey. His diabolical plan is to either stop us or slow us down from reaching our godly aspirations. Here are what appears to be his major areas of attack extracted from the attack launched against Job.

Job's crisis had a domino effect on his life beginning with the "impact of sudden fear" which can also affect our lives in similar ways.

- **The "Sudden Impact of Fear" (Emotional Trauma)**

    In chapter fourteen of the Book of Job, verse one, Job is debating or shall I say, arguing his case before one of his associates, Zopher. He rebuts Zopher's argument by saying, *"Man, born of woman, lives but a few days, and they are full of trouble."* In defense of his claim of innocence, he is saying that all humanity is born into this world plagued with some form of trouble and trauma that's out of their control and can't be explained. When we look at life from the human perspective, we would have to agree and say "He's right."

    The etymology of the word "trouble" there, in the Hebrew language, is associated with "sudden fear" that oppresses the person. **There is an element of surprise and shock associated with major problems in life which is the fear of the unknown.** God knows the unknown, so the key to overcoming the sudden impact of fear is relying upon the Lord to get you through your problem. It's just that simple. However, the pain of *sudden fear* can have a domino effect and lead to other problems like a broken heart.

- **The "Sudden Impact of a Broken Heart" (A Crushed Heart)**

The word "trouble" in the literal Hebrew language of what is considered the Old Testament means that you feel "crowded" in by the "pressure" of external conditions. It means that circumstances and people have imposed upon you that can feel suffocating. That kind of pressure can squeeze the life out of your spiritual heart which can affect your natural heart leading to one giving up on life; even strokes and heart attacks. That's also the nature of a **broken heart**.

A heart can only be broken by someone who gets into your head. When you open your heart to a person, you reveal your inner secret feelings and thoughts. What you said can then be used by the other person against you as they distort your story. Then you can become obsessed with thoughts about that person, whether they "really" love you or care for you. Think about that for a moment . . . I would often illustrate the difference between transparency and gullibility by saying that I can reach into my chest, pull out my heart, and show it. That's transparency. But gullibility that leads to a broken heart reaches into the chest, pulls out the heart, and puts it into the hands of someone to crush. We must balance our feelings between head and heart so that we may have clarity in decision-making.

Don't put your heart into any person's hands. That is, we cannot completely trust any human being. It doesn't mean to be cynical

about people. In the words of Scripture, it means to "guard your heart." *"Guard your heart with all vigilance, for from it are the sources of life.* **(Proverbs 4:23). Only put your heart into the Hands of the Lord.**

When you put your heart into the hands of any person you will begin to wonder if they really love you and if you can trust them. That's especially true when you have opened your soul to them but they haven't opened up to you. When that happens, if you get a "Dear John" letter and they walk away from you, it will leave you feeling empty because they took something from you when they left. They took a piece of your heart and only the Lord can give you a heart transplant or a new heart to fill that void they left in you. A broken heart is hard to recoup from unless the Lord fills that void.

Given the words and behavior of Job's wife, do you think Job had a broken heart? Do you think his wife was influenced by the devil because she uttered pretty much the same words as Satan stated in Job 2:9. *"Then his wife said to him, "Are you still holding firmly to your integrity? Curse God, and die!"* Now listen to his reply to her in verse 10: *"But he replied, "You're talking like one of the godless women would do! Should we receive what is good from God, and not also receive what is evil? In all this Job did not sin by what he said."*

Although Job said *"Receive what is evil from the Lord,"* we know by comparison and consistency of Scripture and God's nature of goodness and holiness that evil does not come from the Lord. It was a true statement recorded by a Scribe, but it wasn't the truth of what was happening. It was Satan launching the attack and it was God who won the victory for Job.

When God sovereignly permits evil to happen there will always be a way out because the purpose was also to expose the evil. Evil is exposed in the aftermath of our trials as in Job's case. (Hindsight Is 20/20 Vision) **Impending trouble and trauma in that case is about God getting rid of the old and getting ready to give you something new.** So, don't give up on people and good times.

- **The "Sudden Impact of Bankruptcy" (Financial Trauma)**

Job experienced instant bankruptcy—he suddenly went from hero to zero.

Can you dare to imagine waking up one morning and going online and discovering that your bank accounts reflect zero, credit cards canceled, your house foreclosed on, your cars repossessed, and all your assets confiscated to pay for loans that were defaulted, and your wife (or husband) and children were gone?

Your first impulse would be, what happened because you didn't think you caused it? Next, you would have to figure out immediately where you would live. You would be out on the streets and flat-broke. Job's sudden disasters and instant bankruptcy were very similar to the previous scenario. Can you imagine the panic and anxiety that he may have been feeling? All his children were dead, his wife seemingly forsook him, his household servants were gone, his friends turned their backs on him, and all his livestock was gone, destroying his livelihood. **Despite the pain** of his crisis, listen to his response. Job 1: 20-22:

Then Job got up and tore his robe. He shaved his head, and then he threw himself down with his face to the ground.

He said, "Naked I came from my mother's womb, and naked I will return there. The Lord gives, and the Lord takes away. May the name of the Lord be blessed!"

In all this Job did not sin, nor did he charge God with moral impropriety.[

His verbal response to his disastrous crisis is a true statement because the Scribe recorded what he said. But because he did not see Satan behind his ordeal, what he said wasn't exactly true. The truth was Satan launched the attack on his household and later it would be God who would restore what he lost.

- **The "Sudden Impact of Sickness and Disease" (Physical Trauma)**

Aside from Satan's bacterial virus infection inflicted on Job, resulting in what appeared to be an incurable disease, Job's financial woes undoubtedly had a negative toxic effect on his health. *"A feast is made for laughter, wine makes life merry, and money is the answer for everything"* (Ecclesiastes 10:19).

According to Scripture, history, and life's experiences, cash, money, and credit are the "basic" necessities of life. Without them, life is a struggle, health is unchecked, and mortality decreases significantly. So, you see the significance of money in life. Here's the point: Although the debilitating terminal disease came from Satan, he was left broke, so even if there was a cure available, he would not have been able to afford it.

Satan's challenge to his health was that he would give everything to live and cease to serve God in exchange for his life. The question is, "Would we give everything for a cure if we were dying?" But God said he couldn't touch his life, so Job wasn't going to die, but he didn't know that. That's the point: Our lives are in God's Hands regardless of the circumstances.

Job sat in the scorching sun like it was chemo therapy while scraping sore boils from his body with a broken piece of pottery. If you have ever had a debilitating terminal disease, you know what trauma feels like in the body. But even in the face of impending death, Job was saying (with the hope of God's Promise) that his eternal state would far outweigh his riches in this life or anything he lost. *"If a man dies, shall he live again? All the days of my hard service* (Appointed Time) *I will wait, Till my change comes"* (Job 14:14 NKJV).

For Job, his losses became a fresh start.

- **The "Sudden Impact of Broken Relationships" (Toxic Relationships)**

    Job's financial state and health condition undoubtedly affected his relationships. Major problems can have a traumatizing effect on relationships. (Finances are one of the main causes of divorce.)

    Traumatic relationships can be substantial, leaving lasting damage, unless treated. **In other words, the damage from toxic/broken relationships can**

arrest one's human development called stunted growth. When one's growth is stunted, it leads to immaturity. Then decisions become delayed which can keep a person in a toxic relationship because the other person got into their heads (gaslighting), making the person think that they are the blame for the problem.

Remember, Job's physical problems were initiated from the spiritual realm, which means the treatment must first be spiritual in nature, followed by therapy suitable to their condition. (Faith and Science can work hand-in-hand.).

Satan's aim in the physical world is to traumatize through trouble because it shocks and paralyzes the person temporarily. The duration of our traumas is determined by our willingness to use our spiritual tools in our toolbox of "Soteriology" (Salvation: Repentance, Forgiveness, Confession, Renouncing) to offset the effects of spiritual attack. But character (the fruit of the Spirit) is the driving force behind overcoming spiritual attack. *"For in Christ Jesus neither circumcision nor uncircumcision carries any weight—**the only thing that matters is faith working through love**"* (Galatians 5:6). There is no slick formula necessary or an exorcism needed to cast the devil out, other than faith in the Lord's provisions.

- **The "Sudden Impact of Death & Dying" (Missing In Action)**

Remember, physiological and psychological pain are signs that we are dying to live. Emphasis is on living, so we must fight through the hurt and pain of discomfort.

Death and dying is a grieving process. Grief is accompanied by great sorrow followed by the expression of mourning. How grief is expressed depends on cultural norms. Notice how Job expressed his grief. He stared death in the face, looked beyond the thin veil between life and death, and anticipated life after death. The point here is grieving and mourning during death and dying for a Believer is about their hopes for a Great Family Reunion, if the other person is a believer too.

When I was diagnosed with prostate cancer in 2019, my immediate thoughts were on a pathogen—something deadly in my body that could kill me.

My initial impulse was not to fear dying. The reason was that three months earlier, while under my gazebo in prayer and meditation, the Lord revealed to me that I would encounter cancer, but it would be like a bump in the road, a hiccup that would resound to God's glory and my greater good.

When I went into surgery to have my prostate removed, I was filled with the anticipation of healing that reflected on my countenance. Long story short, since then, there has been no trace of cancer in my system. Why? I trusted the promise of God and the physicians. But even in the face of the possible loss of my life, like Job, I was thinking that my blissful eternal state would be far better than anything in this life. So, I was ready to face the other possibility.

My greatest concern about death isn't pain or not knowing where I am going. I believe I know where I'm going. What pains me the most is leaving my wife and children because the Lord blessed me to be a stalwart among them. So, my point here is, that we must leave our families a legacy that passes on security for this life and the life to come. Security is more than money. It also involves the knowledge of being a good person who did their level best for their family. But most importantly, it is a legacy of the family continuing in the things of the Lord. You can call it "generational wealth," but most people do not have wealth to pass on. Most people have minimal life insurance or no life insurance at all. You decide what that is. Job's legacy as a good man was intact.

The idea behind Satan's spiritual attacks is to influence one's thinking and dictate their behavior. **Here's how spiritual attack looks from Scripture:**

Character or the "fruit of the Spirit" is a key indicator of a true disciple from a false disciple! Character in the Spirit then becomes the major weapon that overcomes the devil's attacks.

Spiritual Cleansing:

I wrote a paper entitled, *Deliverance versus Spiritual Cleansing*. A true believer cannot be demon-possessed because God and the Devil do not occupy the same space. Nonetheless, a believer can be demonized or influenced in their thinking and sometimes behavior. As far as exorcism goes, Hollywood is the creator and provocateur of the idea of that kind of demonic possession. Scripturally, demonic possession is an affliction that distorts and perverts human behavior. The difference is some people who are captured by spiritual forces are functional in society. That's where demonic attack is a form of deception that creates delusions of the mind making the person think in a way of an alternate reality. **Let's look at it in juxtaposition (side-by-side) to know the difference.**

—*Precaution*—

When it comes to dealing with and ministering to believers' or non-believers' spiritual condition, keep in mind that Christ is the key to their cleansing, deliverance, and recovery.

When confronting a non-believer in outreach ministry, the first recourse is to gain their permission to introduce them to Christ. They should be led in the "prayer of faith" to accept and receive the Lord as their "personal" Saviour. If they refuse, there is nothing else that can be done because Christ must be invited and received into their hearts. In the case of a believer plagued by demonic attack, the first step is to make sure that the person is assured that Christ is in their life. If they are sure or unsure, either way, someone should lead them into a prayer of assurance.

Non-Believers

Scripturally, there are three levels of Satanic attacks on non-Christians.

- **Obsession.** Reoccurring thoughts.

- **Oppression.** Compelling bizarre expressions and behavior that are uncontrollable.

- **Possession.** Occupancy of the mind that can control the body. Can also equate to insanity.

Believers

Scripturally there are two levels of Satanic attack on a Christian's life.

- **Obsession.** Reoccurring thoughts.

- **Oppression.** Uncontrollable Bad Habits that must be renounced.

- **True Believers cannot be possessed by demons.**

The results of this spiritual exercise depend on "their" faith perspective, not "your" perspective of faith. So make sure the prayer focuses on Christ and redemption.

If you believe that one can lose their salvation at some point, and the Spirit of God leaves them, and then a foreign spirit comes and occupies that space, then more than likely, you believe that a Christian can be demon-possessed. Your understanding of that more than likely comes from teachings about Mathew 12:43-45 where Christ gives a parable (fictitious story used as a metaphor) about healing and casting the devil out. The point is, when an unregenerate (non-Christian) person is delivered from the clutches of the devil, they should immediately receive the Lord as their "personal" Saviour. If they don't, they will have an empty heart that is vulnerable to more demonic spirits to return and make things worse than before. The parable does not apply to being saved and then unsaved.

Salvation isn't sporadic or random, it's permanent. Scripture says "He will never leave us or forsake us but will be with us until the end of the age." (Matthew 28:20; Hebrews 13:5). If we can lose our salvation, tell me at what point do we lose it and where do we draw the line?

Nevertheless, if you believe that a Christian cannot lose their salvation at any point, you tend to believe that a Christian cannot be demon-possessed. But, always call on the Lord first in times of trouble!

because if you confess with your mouth that Jesus is Lord and believe in your heart that God raised him from the dead, you will be saved.

For with the heart one believes and thus has righteousness and with the mouth one confesses and thus has salvation.

For the scripture says, "Everyone who believes in him will not be put to shame."

For there is no distinction between the Jew and the Greek, for the same Lord is Lord of all, who richly blesses all who call on him.

For everyone who calls on the name of the Lord will be saved (Romans 10:9-13).

NEXT: *Scars of War: Old Wounds*

CHAPTER 6

Scars of War: Old Wounds!!!

Chapter Overview

Here, we begin by looking at what delays and hinders our healing which is the "sin syndrome" (symptoms of sin consciousness) which is the person's misconstrued view of the meaning of sin. (Knowing the truth about sin eliminates any excuses that we have to follow the Lord.) We point out "why" all humanity is broken and imperfect and how God "works through" broken imperfect people in ministry. Rather than using the term "uses" because it can be a violation of free will, we look at how God works through broken vessels. Broken people become wounded healers. We look at biblical examples of brokenness and the ultimate Wounded Healer, the Lord, and end with the statement that our emotional/spiritual scars are a Badge of Honor!

"Nobody escapes being wounded. We all are wounded people, whether physically, emotionally, mentally, or spiritually. The main question is not "How can we hide our wounds?" so we don't have to be embarrassed, but "How can we put our woundedness in the service of others?" When our wounds cease to be a source of shame, and become a source of healing, we have become wounded healers. (Henri J.M. Nouwen- https://www.goodreads.com/quotes/8383040)

Wounded Healers in Scripture are believers who acknowledge their imperfections and shortcomings. But they do not allow their failures to stop their progress of growth and development toward Christ-likeness. So, let me, in retrospect, give an insightful definition of sin here. The idea is to point out that the main hindrance to resisting God working through us is the "sin syndrome" (symptoms of sin consciousness):

> [The etymology of the word sin in both Hebrew and Greek means to *fall short* by *transgressing* the *revealed will* of God. Note, once again, the "revealed will" of God. Why? Because God doesn't hold us accountable for something we don't know. That wouldn't be just or fair. But what we know of the *virtues* of the Lord (that was translated and paraphrased as morals) is recorded in the Ten Commandments. Together it means if our conscience is "convicted" when violating the virtues of the Lord, we have sinned. But if we are unaware that we are violating the virtues of the Lord, we may have appeared to sin in the view of people, but not in the Eyes of God (God winks at our ignorance—Acts 17:31-32).

> To obey or disobey God is determined by whether God revealed the Word of the Lord to you by the Spirit of God called the *Rhema Word* in Matthew 4:4, "... *It is written,* **'Man does not live by bread alone, but by every word that comes from the mouth of God.**" The word "word" is *rhema* and means God-breathed into one's consciousness.

> The word that was translated from Koine Greek to English for sin is *Harmartia* and it "actually" comes from the experience of an archer shooting at a target. If the archer completely missed the target the spotter would cry out "harmartia," meaning, you missed the

mark. So, simply, sin means to miss the mark by refusing to obey the revealed will of God. **(The Diagram in the Conclusion can help to understand the "sin nature."]**

Knowing the truth about sin eliminates any excuses that we have to follow the Lord. Your idea and concept of sin should not be a hindrance or stop you from serving the Lord. The Scriptural truth is that God works best through broken vessels. Broken vessels have repented and humbled themselves and are consequently, more open and willing for God to work through them. Besides, the word itself "use" implies manipulation and God does not manipulate free will. Free will must be open to the Lord, granting God access to using the broken vessel . . . The bottom line is, you don't have to be an ordained minister, title holder, or a professional for God to work through you. Also, the broken vessels that God works through can be any color, creed, culture, rich, poor, male, female, young, or old. God doesn't discriminate. When a person is healed from the pain of their trauma they become empathetic to similar problems in others.

****

A wounded healer sounds as though a person remains in a broken state as God uses them. No, a believer doesn't stay wounded. We sustain injuries but are made whole again. With each hurting experience, we become stronger. *"But he said to me, "My grace is enough for you, for my power is made perfect in weakness* (2 Corinthians 12:9a).

In my efforts to reach people with the "Good News" of a transformed life through the Lord, the main excuse that I would hear from them was, "I'm not ready." They are saying they are "not" ready to give up their particular sins. The truth is that God does not save us when we clean up first. That would mean we are saved by our "own" efforts and the good things we do. Salvation is not "earned" by the "good" things we do. Salvation is by grace alone produced by Christ's finished work on the cross. *"For it is by grace you have been saved, through faith—and this is not from yourselves, it is the gift of God—"* (Ephesians 2:8).

Christ merited God's favor to bless us with the gift of salvation because we don't deserve it and can't earn our way to heaven. We must "invite" Christ into our hearts as our salvation and passage to heaven. God's Salvation is a complete package for eternal life and for God working through us. God can use us in our imperfect state, and as God uses us to help others, we will improve. WE GROW AS WE GO!

The point is, they saw the Christian life as an ideal that they could not live up to because they were still doing wrong things and were not suitable. In other words, they saw the Christian life as a hard life to live. The proverbial saying that came from that notion to rebut that excuse was, "It's like scaling a fish before you catch it" which is impossible. You have to catch the fish first.

The "raw" truth is that all humanity was born with a "fallen" nature and consequently, broken. The "good news" is, the Lord redeemed us from our fallen state, but the residue of places of brokenness remains in the life of a believer like leftover baggage. However, it doesn't mean that we cannot come to the Lord with all our imperfections and struggles to live a better life. Before returning to the tragedies of Job, let me give you some Scriptural examples of "why" and "how" God works through "broken vessels."

GOD WORKS THROUGH BROKEN VESSELS

Let me give you a Scriptural analogy of the effects of brokenness that God uses to shine the light of the Lord. I call it "Broken Vessels and Shining Lights."

In Judges 6:11, Gideon, a young farm boy, was called by God to defeat Israel's enemies, the Philistines. But he was very skeptical because he didn't have the age, title, training, or ability to defeat such a formidable army. Like others in the nation, he was afraid of them because of their stature and weapons of warfare, so God found him hiding in a wine press, threshing wheat. The truth is, he would not have been the first choice of those who were part of Israel's army to undertake such an enormous task, but he was God's choice.

Throughout Scripture, (Although there were exceptions to the rule like the Apostle Paul.) the men and women that God chose to anoint for victory against their enemies did not "fit the bill." They would be considered unqualified in human terms. But God does not see people like people see people. God looks at the heart and chooses people from the heart. God's choice was not based on their physical appearance or status in life. One example is David who became King but appeared to be unqualified compared to his brothers. Thus, God's words to Samuel about the criteria of selection: *"But the Lord said to Samuel, 'Don't be impressed by his appearance or his height, for I have rejected him. God does not view things the way people do. People look on the outward appearance, but the Lord looks at the heart"* (1 Samuel 16:7). After rejecting David's robust brothers God reveals to Samuel why David was selected: *"After removing Saul, he made David their king. God testified concerning him: 'I have found David son of Jesse, a man after my own heart; he will do everything I want him to do"* (Acts 13:22 NIV).

God chooses human vessels that appear weak, lowly, despised, devalued, seemingly worthless, and unqualified for the assignment. God's infinite reasoning is so that there is no way they can be credited for what happens when they win. Rather, God gets the credit and glory (1 Corinthians 1:20-31).

Long story short, Gideon tried to get out of what God called him to do because he saw himself as unqualified too. That is until God confirmed his call through signs. Then he was TESTED at the brook by God to determine his level of commitment . . . (Judges 6). He passes the test. But then God makes his task look even harder because he is reduced to having just 300 men instead of the 32,000 that he started with. The point is, God doesn't need as many people against you as your enemies. Why? Because the most important battle is waged in the heavenlies where God's angels defeat your spiritual enemies behind your physical foes. (One will put 1000 to flight; two will put 10,000 to flight—Deuteronomy 32:30)

The formula for Gideon's victory was simple: God instructed him to give each man a water pitcher and to put a torch on the inside in one hand and a trumpet in the other hand (Judges 7:19). Then once all three bands of men surrounded the camp of their enemies at a vulnerable time of the morning (around 2:00 am), they were to (in order) break the pitcher exposing glaring light from the torch. Then blow the trumpet and shout, "The sword of the Lord and for Gideon." The result in the early morning was chaos and the light blinded them. The trumpet frightened them and scattered them because it sounded like there were more men than they had against them. With his victory, he went into the "Hero Judges" Hall of Fame.

The point is, in the Hands of God, we are like Gideon. God works through broken vessels to demonstrate His glory that will contribute to our greater good.

—Broken People Are Wounded Healers—

I've often quoted Henry Houwen's "Wounded Healer" to point out how I see broken vessels or imperfect people with flaws. But now I see things a little differently. Previously, I saw wounded healers as people in a perpetual state of brokenness. But now (after some critical thinking, analysis, and study and experience in life) if that's the case for wounded healers, when do they heal to serve other broken people? Noncritically, I don't think that two alcoholics or drug addicts can "really" help each other. Consequently, my concept of wounded healers is sequential. That is, those who follow the Lord experience brokenness and then heal in the area of brokenness, then go on to be healed in another area of their lives. It means that we do not reach perfection in this life. But we do climb from plateaus of spiritual growth to plateaus of spiritual growth that impact our maturation. **Instead, it implies a perpetual state of healing rather than a perpetual state of brokenness.**

The experience of problems and troubles that we must overcome enables the believer to become empathetic to those they serve who experienced similar things. Job's experience with brokenness enabled him to forgive his "haters" because he saw his "own" weakness and healed. This means that we are healing while we serve. But, caution, when we are healing we must stay away from people and circumstances that make our weaknesses vulnerable to temptation.

—Job: The Wounded Healer—

"Again the day came when the sons of God came to present themselves before the Lord, and Satan also arrived among them to present himself before the Lord.

And the Lord said to Satan, "Where have you come from?" Satan answered the Lord, "From roving about on the earth, and from walking back and forth across it."

> *Then the Lord said to Satan, "Have you considered my servant Job? For there is no one like him on the earth, a pure and upright man, one who fears God and turns away from evil. And he still holds firmly to his integrity, so that you stirred me up to destroy him without reason."*
>
> *But Satan answered the Lord, "Skin for skin! Indeed, a man will give up all that he has to save his life.*
>
> *But extend your hand and strike his bone and his flesh, and he will no doubt curse you to your face!"*
>
> *So the Lord said to Satan, "All right, he is in your power; only preserve his life."*
>
> *So Satan went out from the presence of the Lord, and he afflicted Job with a malignant ulcer from the soles of his feet to the top of his head.*
>
> *Job took a shard of broken pottery to scrape himself with while he was sitting among the ashes (Job 2:1-8).*

One can speculate that Job developed a form of skin cancer and (ironically) sat in the scorching sun as a means of radiation treatment that may have prolonged his life. Despite the "fictional faith" views that separate faith from medicine and science, science and the remedies of God on earth (in all of nature) can prevent and cure ailments. That is the basis of medical research and breakthroughs.

You can only imagine the lives Job changed through recovery from his ordeal. His physical and emotional pain was so severe that at one point, he wished to be miscarried before birth or die in infancy (Job 3:1-7). He wanted to die as a means of getting rid of his pain and suffering— Euthanasia. Life can become so bad for some people that they develop a death wish when God says "LIVE."

Some of us may have a problem with understanding the concept of "Wounded but Healing" because human

nature strives to avoid pain and seek pleasure. But this is where the divine connects with the human.

The idea here means that you don't have to be a perfect person for God to work through you. Just be available and willing, with an open heart.

—*The Lord: The Ultimate Wounded Healer*—

Jesus is our Wounded Healer: *"Through His wounds, we are healed. Jesus suffering and death brought joy and life. His humiliation brought glory; his rejection brought a community of love. As followers of Jesus, we can also allow our wounds to bring healing to others"* (Henri J.M. Nouwen).

*"He was despised and rejected by people,
one who experienced pain and was acquainted with illness;
people hid their faces from him; he was despised, and we considered him insignificant.*

*But he lifted up our illnesses,
he carried our pain;
even though we thought he was being punished, attacked by God, and afflicted for something he had done.*

*He was wounded because of our rebellious deeds,
crushed because of our sins;
he endured punishment that made us well; because of his wounds we have been healed* (Isaiah 53:3-5).

"The Messiah is no magician. He does not wave a magic wand and all of our problems disappear. He's no genie in a lamp. He's not a fairytale or fantasy . . . He takes care of the sick one by one, wound by wound, bruise by bruise, sore by sore, bandage by bandage. The Messiah

is a healer of men and women." (Excerpt from "The Way of the Heart" by Henri J.M. Nouwen)

My conclusion about Isaiah 53:5 is that it is often misquoted by the hyper-spiritual "name it, claim it, it's yours" group. They quote the verse above like some formula for healing the body even when they are sick and have no indication of healing. Then when their symptoms and condition worsen, they blame God without saying it, and their faith is "shipwrecked."

However, Isaiah 53:5 isn't figurative language either. Nor are they "hot air" words uttered to some visualized chanting as an illusion of physical healing. It is the focus of our spiritual healing from a fallen life. It means that through God's judicial system of "justification," legally, we are whole in the Eyes of God. The Scriptural context and prescription for our healing come directly from the Lord, our High Priest, *"touched with the feelings of our infirmities." "For we do not have a high priest incapable of sympathizing with our weaknesses, but one who has been tempted in every way just as we are, yet without sin* (Hebrews 4:15). **Healing Comes From God's Virtues— Attributes of God's Nature Beginning With Love.** *"And the whole multitude sought to touch him: for there went virtue out of him, and healed them all* (Luke 6:19 KJV).

****

Depending on the severity of a physical injury or wound, some wounds can leave a permanent scar. That scar becomes a constant reminder of what caused the scar. It can also be triggered by similar incidents. Likewise, emotional and spiritual injuries can leave an internal scar on the soul. It also becomes a reminder of what caused the scar that can be triggered. When it is triggered the person will shut down, blocking communication, or snap mentally and emotionally. That scar is usually still festering and like a physical injury, it needs treatment.

There isn't much we can do about a severe physical scar, even with plastic surgery. But, the scars of emotional and spiritual injuries can be healed and removed. But the festering bandages must be removed first. We must acknowledge the pain and the source to remove the bandage.

Some of us (outwardly) don't look like what our wounds and injuries have inflicted or what we have gone through in life because they are hidden on the inside. We wear masks to mask our pain. But caution here. Those bandages should be removed confidentially, one-on-one in the presence of a qualified counselor, preferably a therapist.

Wounds kept untreated can fester physically, mentally, and emotionally. In other words, the traumatic problems of the past can linger. To properly treat those wounds, the bandages that we use to hide the wounds must be removed, exposing the wound for proper treatment. That hurts but heals!

Our Emotional/Spiritual Scars Are A Badge Of Honor!

According to historians of Scripture, the Apostle Paul, selected by the Lord Himself to replace Judas Iscariot, was disfigured from the injuries he sustained due to persecution. The persecution rendered him not so pleasant to look at. He was also the most literary of all-inspired writers of Scripture. He wrote more books than any other. But it all came with a price that ultimately took his life. However, he never looked at his suffering and pain as defeat! He saw his suffering and pain as a means of spreading the gospel as stated in "Foxes Book of Martyrs": *"The Blood of Martyrs is the Seed of the Church"* (Tertullian-Early Church Father).

When it came time for Paul to be beheaded as capital punishment for the charge and crime of sedition (*"For we have found this man a pestilent fellow, and a mover of sedition among all the Jews throughout the world, and a ringleader of the sect of the Nazarenes:"*—Acts 24:5), he willingly walked (of his own volition) from his rented apartment jail, and laid his head on the chopping block. Before his martyrdom, he wrote these words: *"For I am now ready to be offered, and the time of my departure is at hand. I have fought a good fight, I have finished my course, I have kept the faith: Henceforth there is laid up for me a crown of righteousness, which the Lord, the righteous judge, shall give me at that day: and not to me only, but unto all them also that love his appearing"* (2 Timothy 4:6-8).

Let me say here that authentic followers of the Lord (disciples) are not popular among institutionalized Christians, let alone in the real world. The Apostle Paul referred to his persecution coming from within and without (2 Corinthians 7:5).

But we have this treasure in clay jars, so that the extraordinary power belongs to God and does not come from us.

We are experiencing trouble on every side, but are not crushed; we are perplexed, but not driven to despair;

we are persecuted, but not abandoned; we are knocked down, but not destroyed,

always carrying around in our body the death of Jesus, so that the life of Jesus may also be made visible in our body (2 Corinthians 4:7-10).

His disfiguring physical scars and an eye condition that dimmed his vision came from his sufferings for the Lord. But he wore them as a badge of honor and privilege to walk in the footsteps of the Lord. *"From now on let no one cause me trouble, for I bear the marks of Jesus on my body"* (Galatians 6:17).

NEXT: *Finding Purpose—God's Pre-Ordained Plan*

CHAPTER 7

Finding Purpose: God's Pre-Ordained Plan!!!

Chapter Overview

We begin by looking at how God builds the Kingdom of God on this renovated earth through time up to the Regeneration. "Personal" convictions become the unction and the prodding drive to building God's agenda in our lives. Emphasis is on how God builds the Kingdom in us and how we follow through by building the Kingdom around us and within the community of service. To effectively build God's Kingdom, begins with a consideration of our responsibility. It means that our role and responsibility in any problem is for a TESTIMONY to God's Glory and our greater good. Our purpose is in our testimony and our testimony is in our calling, so find your calling. Generally, the calling of every Believer is to proclaim and promote the Kingdom of God by sharing their faith when necessary. It discloses the secret private places of the heart that must be open to the Lord for deliverance and recovery. (Spiritual Discipline Balances Life And Aids Your Purpose But Discipline Is Not Punishment.) The chapter concludes with an analysis of the "fruit of the Spirit" as qualities of a believer's character. Here you will discover what it means to love your enemies and how reciprocity (sowing and reaping) works.

God's sovereign eternal plans run from Genesis to Revelation 21-22. That plan and purpose is to build the Kingdom of God on earth. I know how that sounds to the carnal mind, like some kind of fairytale. But to the spiritual mind and astute student of Scripture, it is the coming reality that will be announced by the appearance of the Lord. So, when prayerfully soul-searching for God's purpose and plans for your life, think hard about what you are building for the Lord through your life by your "personal convictions." Your "personal" convictions are at the core of what you believe and what you are most sensitive about.

****

If you can believe it, Job's claim to innocence slowed the process of healing, recovery, and restoration. Or, do you think that everything is on God's timetable and we have no responsibility for how, when, where, why, and by whom something happens? Remember the chess game? Also, fate is in your hands, but destiny is in God's Hands. So, we have a role for things happening, not just everybody else. We bear some of the responsibility, but not all. My point is, Job's recovery was associated with him discovering God's purpose in his ordeal and crisis.

That was the purpose of God confronting Job from within the vision of the tornado; to help him see himself in the mirror of God's vast Creation. Can you see yourself when you look into the mirror of God's Creation displayed in God's Word? Job saw himself when God spoke and reproved him out of the vision of the tornado.

Could Job have been arrogant with selective amnesia like people today? I think so. (Selective amnesia can be influenced by trauma or severe pain that is blocked out of the memory.) I'm painting a fully human image of Job because it's all there in Scripture if we know how to connect the dots by comparing Scripture and human nature.

Just as the first man in his humanity and free will chose to disobey God for a reason, regardless of the reason, he bore the brunt of the responsibility. The point is, throughout history and Scripture no one is perfect and everyone has made some mistakes in life that they are not proud of and that they regret. I'm not proud of everything that happened in my life. But neither am I ashamed of those things because I'm forgiven and my heart has been cleansed. So, I'll rephrase the saying by saying, that everyone regrets something when they don't know their purpose.

When you know your destiny, everything in your life has a purpose and meaning. But God's desire is not to condemn us for what happens, but to override the problem through eternal forgiveness to compensate us for our sacrifice. Yes, our sincere acknowledgments from a broken and contrite heart become the acceptable sacrifices of worship that God will compensate.

After God gets through chiding Job, he sees himself in the mirror of infinite eternity and is convicted about how small and insignificant he was in the scheme of God's Creation.

HYPOTHETICALLY IMAGINE GOD SAYING: Job, it's not about you. It's about Me and My purpose and plan for My world. You have a role and responsibility, to *present*, *promote*, and *proclaim* Who "I Am." **There it is.** But how many are living beneath that privilege in name only? That's our purpose that lays out God's pre-ordained plan for our lives. That was Job's responsibility, and he was successful in the end. But it was a struggle to get there. Are you willing to claim your purpose through struggle? Let me explain with an illustration:

The most brilliant, beautiful, smooth stones were made by constant pounding of water over time. So to speak, when we stand under the providential flow of God's Word upon our human spirit, the rough edges are made smooth and, like stones standing under the pounding of water, the dirt and debris are moved out from our lives revealing a beautiful heart. It's not as daunting as it sounds and is a simple matter of walking by faith with the Lord. As a believer, just live your normal life and listen to your heart's instructions.

Think of that for a moment . . . Regardless of what we go through in life (bad or good), as Believers, is to live up to our Savior's calling. So, don't be afraid of the truth no matter how it hurts! THE TRUTH WILL ALWAYS WIN WHEN IT IS TIME TESTED. Ah, but know that people will perceive your testimony as real or false, or they may use what you share in your testimony to bring up your past for judgment. Either way, the end product of your testimony proclaims loudly the glory of the Lord. So Raise Your Voice about the Goodness of the Lord! Take the narrative and conversation of life out of the political arena, change the religious jargon, and speak plainly about Kingdom Concepts that stand above religion politics, and societal norms.

Our calling is our purpose in life, and besides clergy, every believer has a calling to represent the Lord by their testimony. *"But they overcame him by the blood of the Lamb and by the word of their testimony, and they did not love their lives so much that they were afraid to die."* (Revelation 12:11).

As trivial as it may sound, was Job, due to his self-righteousness and assuming innocence, partially responsible for his trial? People commonly imply that the problems we face are a matter of our choice. But some problems in life are out of our control. Some bad decisions are a matter of human weakness. So, the fault of mistakes is a decision we live with, but the focus should not be on blame, but rather, on how one can bounce back from the bad decision. **Remember, the past can not be changed, but we can change today.**

****

Job's problems are initiated in the spiritual realm and so can ours and result in trouble or trauma. Let's talk about how that realm can "possibly" look from various Scripture and how it functions when it comes to our troubles.

I think everyone can agree that there are natural human influencers. But do we believe that there are spiritual influencers behind some human influence? I posed that question when I opened Job's crisis and calamity with the conversation between God and Satan. Do you believe that what we say and do can be influenced by God or the devil? Let's look at what happened with Job and you can decide for yourself.

First, think about this: Metaphorically, it is ridiculous and ludicrous that God would fight physical battles with human beings. Even if it were possible it would result in a fire that would consume God's opposition in the blink of an eye. It would not even be a battle. **God fights spiritual battles in the spiritual realm with the angels of God fighting on behalf of their assigned believer which will affect human life.**

When Satan's emissaries are defeated by God's angels in the spiritual realm the resistance to our problems weakens. Then a door is opened for us to proceed into God's exponential blessings. The spiritual forces that stand in our way have been removed. But, take heed, they can come back with a "vengeance" if we revert to the people and things that got us in trouble.

Take a look at what happened with Job. Once Job authorized heaven to release him from being held hostage by his acknowledgment and repentance, God turned his captivity and God will do the same for us if we believe. It doesn't require any rigamarole or spiritual calisthenics, speaking in erratic tongues, or having hands (that God knows been where) laid on your head. **It becomes a simple act of "Yielding" for God to intervene.**

As odd as it sounds, realistically, God in our hearts is not enough to fight spiritual battles. Listen carefully to this: God must also be "invited" not only into our hearts but into our outward circumstances and the "affairs" of our lives to defeat our spiritual enemies. But most people are afraid of that because they don't want to let go of the pleasures of sin, lasciviousness. As worldly as it sounds, we must allow God to meddle in our business. No place in our lives is off-limits for God. To correct our lives we must consciously turn those matters over to the Lord. It doesn't mean we stop working on those things. **It means that God becomes our partner to solve those difficulties.**

The hard truth is that everyone has secrets that individuals disclose to no one. The reason they are undisclosed and kept in the inner sanctuaries of our hearts is that we do not believe that people will understand us and condemn us for those inner thoughts. Neither does it mean we are doing the things we are thinking about. They are just embarrassing. No one knows about their "secrets" but that person. The difficulty with that is that no one wants or desires anyone else in their personal private space. I call it the secret chambers of the heart that we don't reveal to anyone because "maybe" what's in there is wrong and embarrassing. But, God isn't like people. God won't spread your business as rumors and gossip. God will forgive, forget, and move us on to the next chapter.

So, when you are done "saying" from your mouth that "The battle is not mine but the Lord's" be prepared for God to crash your party. That is, God, coming into your circumstances by INVITATION that may disrupt your circumstances by shattering them which means things will go wrong for the sake of chasing toxic people away from you. The point is taking a recourse (change of direction) from the course you were headed. NO SURPRISES! That sounds bad but it's "actually" good because God is giving you another chance for a better life. Let the Lord lead and guide you into new relationships and new situations. Can you see that in Job's life?

****

God gave Job more than he had, more children, and possibly a new wife. Job's wife isn't named but after his debilitating, possibly terminal illness, she suddenly appears, not to encourage him but to put him down for holding on to his integrity. Does her sudden appearance after the first wave of his trial indicate that she was not supportive of him throughout his trial? When she sees him sitting in the dust and scraping his sore boils with a broken piece of pottery, she bellows out: *"Do you still persist in your integrity? Curse God, and die"*—Job 2:9).

I have some questions about Job's wife. This, of course, is conjecture based on the common propensity of fallen human nature (What we are subject to do given the right circumstances). Did she just show up after the first wave of Job's trial, which indicates she may have left him when all hell broke out? Do you think Job had a bad marriage? Why? Well, true love doesn't turn against the person they love, especially during a crisis. Why would she speak defamatory words to her husband if she was a loving wife? Does it sound like she was "slapping back" at Job (hand in face) and saying . . .

you're a miserable man. Look at you! You're no good for me or anyone else, so why don't you just die."

Or, do you think that Job's wife had some unmet needs because her husband may have been too busy maintaining business away from home? We "really" don't know the full story of her telling her husband to curse God and die, but it sure sounds like she uttered the same words uttered by Satan to God. So, was she influenced by the devil? Did she leave him after her disparaging words? Did God give Job a new wife? Remember, monogamy was not a law of the land then. Also, possibly he had new friends (Job 42:10-16).

****

The purpose of the life of a Believer (universally and locally) is to "Glorify the Lord." Now that sounds very general and ambiguous. Nonetheless, in practical application, it means to let your faith speak for itself when people question your faith with a direct answer from Scripture. *"But set Christ apart as Lord in your hearts and always be ready to give an answer to anyone who asks about the hope you possess"* (1 Peter 3:15).

The prescription for this is found in this verse: *"In the same way, let your light shine before people, so that they can see your good deeds and give honor to your Father in heaven"* (Matthew 5:16). Although the good that we do does not produce salvation for ourselves, nevertheless, it becomes a means of the "goodness" of the Lord that leads others to salvation.

Light in the previous Scripture means to illuminate the life of Christ in us which is the basis of glorifying the Lord by simply opening our hearts to the Lord. But the question still stands: How do we do that? In the interim of your faith "not" being questioned, live your normal life by reflecting a virtuous character that demonstrates the presence of the Lord in your life. (I'll talk about that soon.) You don't have to pass out tracts or beat people over the head with the Bible to "make" them a Christian to prove you are a Christian.

Purpose Overrides Surprises

When planning whether for life, business, or ministry, we must consider the possible caveats. Caveats are warning signs or admonishments. For a believer, both become convictions of the heart.

Little children, let us not love with word or with tongue but in deed and truth.

(Remember my points concerning virtues of the heart that produce Christ-like character? In that context, virtues are not emotions but spiritual qualities of the heart that we must yield to. Those virtues are referred to as the "fruit of the Spirit"—Galatians 5: 22-23 that will be elaborated as spiritual disciplines in the life of a believer.)

And by this we will know that we are of the truth and will convince our conscience in his presence,

that if our conscience condemns us, that God is greater than our conscience and knows all things.

Dear friends, if our conscience does not condemn us, we have confidence in the presence of God,

and whatever we ask we receive from him, because we keep his commandments and do the things that are pleasing to him.

And the person who keeps his commandments resides in God, and God in him. Now by this we know that God resides in us: by the Spirit he has given us (1 John 3:18-22).

—*Spiritual Discipline Balances Life And Aids Your Purpose*—

My analogy of balance is like equilibrium in the mind and body. When the body's equilibrium is off, it causes dizziness and unbalance. When a Believer's life is out of balance, it causes confusion and uncertainty, leading to a sporadic life (Double-Mindedness).

We learn how to walk by faith in the real world, not the church world, through everyday occurrences. The Lord has strengthened my walk with Him where I strike a balance between an uncompromised faith when I am out there in the real world and a non-condemning view of the people. That is my moderation.

I think the key is getting closer to the Lord because His love emanates through trouble. Paul indicates in *Romans 5:1-5* that the results of our **trouble** are a growing experience that brings out of us the love of God! By comparison with other Scripture, it means that God's nature, which is love, is planted within our spirit like a seed and grows within our personalities.

Romans 5:1-5 is also a prescription (meant to be applied) that puts our progression towards Christlikeness in relevant terms. Here's how our progression looks in chronological order through the application of the passage above: **First**, verse two states that we have **access** to the Throne of Grace for God's unmerited favor to meet our needs to glorify the Lord. **Second**, it indicates that God's grace will sustain us in suffering by producing **endurance**, which means bearing up under pressure. **Third**, it indicates the grace to bear up under pressure will help to shape a Christlike **character**. **Fourth**, the Christlike character will then give us **hope**. And **finally**, hope will render us **unashamed** of what we go through and we will not be **disappointed** (No Surprises!). When added all up, all things being equal, we will come through our trials with **confidence** in the Lord like Daniel and the three Hebrew boys in the Book of Daniel (Their trials were a refining process that set them free). So, let me say this about experience from the passage as I segue into the fruit of the Spirit.

They say that experience is the best teacher but I say that experience with the Lord is the best because we have been given an "unction"; a learning anointing from the Lord (1 John 2:20;27). Experience also aids in the development of the fruit of the Spirit, which isn't **emotions** but **spiritual virtues** of the heart that must be yielded to when facing opposition and obstacles that get in the way of our progression.

"The Fruit of the Spirit"

The *fruit of the spirit* is a discipline or spiritual ability to enhance and develop skills for specific challenges and tasks. **Discipline grants us restraint from bad habits and the drive to pursue good habits for the body, mind, and soul.** It implies that those skills must be practiced like an Olympian.

The *fruit of the Spirit* does not manifest in a worship experience, within fellowship, a seminar, or a teaching session. **The *fruit of the Spirit* will manifest in our walk of faith with the Lord in the real world as we engage in challenges and obstacles as we pursue the cause of Christ.** However, the fruit of the Spirit is a neglected and unpopular conversation piece and teaching in church circles today because it is so foreign to where people live, work, and play. It's a nice topic for study, but far from the daily reality of a person's walk with the Lord.

Like an Olympian, discipline is the form of behavior modification that God uses to train and develop disciples and grow the Lord's people.

—*Discipline is not Punishment*—

I think it's good for Believers to know that God does not punish the People of God which either takes away a privilege or exacts some form of pain. Punishment is condemnation and God does not condemn the People of God ((Romans 8:1-4). The Lord took our pain and punishment on the Cross as our vicarious sufferer and substitute for sin.

There is therefore now no condemnation for those who are in Christ Jesus.

For the law of the life-giving Spirit in Christ Jesus has set you free from the law of sin and death.

For God achieved what the law could not do because it was weakened through the flesh. By sending his own Son in the likeness of sinful flesh and concerning sin, he condemned sin in the flesh,

so that the righteous requirement of the law may be fulfilled in us, who do not walk according to the flesh but according to the Spirit (Romans 8:1-4).

God disciplines us by cleansing us from bad habits that get us in trouble. ***"But if we were more discerning with regard to ourselves, we would not come under such judgment. Nevertheless, when we are judged in this way by the Lord, we are being disciplined so that we will not be finally condemned with the world'* (1 Corinthians 11: 31-32).**

The translated word in English for the Greek word discipline is "chastise," which implies some form of severe punishment like a "whipping." Nevertheless, in real life, when God disciplines us, like a good spanking, it stings by convicting our conscience. The word chastise can be found in the Authorized King James Version of the Bible in Hebrews 12:5-8 to point out how God disciplines:

> *And ye have forgotten the exhortation which speaketh unto you as unto children, My son, despise not thou the chastening of the Lord, nor faint when thou art rebuked of him: for whom the Lord loveth he chasteneth, and scourgeth every son whom he receiveth. If ye endure chastening, God dealeth with you as with sons; for what son is he whom the father chasteneth not? But if ye be without chastisement, whereof all are partakers, then are ye bastards, and not sons.*

Although we view the word "bastard" as a curse word in our evolution of language, coming from the original language it means an illegitimate child. The writer of the Book of Hebrews is making the point that we must experience the "new birth" (John 3:3).

God does not punish people. People punish themselves when they willfully ignore the laws of conscience, also the laws of nature when they dismiss climate change. God warns us of the consequences of the violation of the Moral Law (Ten Commands) and the laws of nature through the decree of judgments.

When Believers are walking in love and love has become part of their character, they have a heartfelt reverence for God, dignity and self-respect, and dignified respect for people. They seek to abide by the laws of conscience and the laws of nature.

The character of respect has been reinforced in my life through my experiences. Outer religious rules and regulations do not penetrate the heart to impact love and respect. The inner work of the *fruit of the Spirit* becomes the inner conviction and guide to obedience that fulfills the Moral Law. ***Romans 13:10b, "...love is the fulfillment of the law."* The Fruit of the Spirit Fortifies the**

Condition of the Heart. Let's take a look at the fruit of the Spirit, fruit by fruit in practical application:

Galatians 5:22-23

Note here that all the virtues of the "Fruit of the Spirit" grow within human character. God's virtues within us become like seeds that are planted that take root and then begin to grow. But to produce a healthy crop a farmer must cultivate and fertilize their crops and they need heat, sunlight, and plenty of water to grow. For the *fruit of the Spirit* to flourish certain circumstances, situations, and people are the cultivating factors like the elements needed in farming. Remember, this approach is a pragmatic application to our lives, and not head knowledge being taught.

But the fruit of the Spirit is:

- ✓ **LOVE, THE HEART'S SECURITY!**

    Coupled with the spiritual soldier's armor of the "Breastplate of Righteousness" recorded in Ephesians 6:14, God's love guards our hearts. God's love is different from human emotional love in that it is unconditional and commits to loving people unemotionally. When we love with God's love from the heart, it is compassion or empathy that identifies with other people's situations and plight like the Lord. *"For we do not have a high priest incapable of sympathizing with our weaknesses, but one who has been tempted in every way just as we are, yet without sin. Therefore let us confidently approach the throne of grace to receive mercy and find grace whenever we need help"* (Hebrews 4:15-16). Also when you are confronted with hate and ridicule for your faith, *"yield"* to the quality of God's love in your heart and do not retort. But say "the Lord rebuke you" as we see in the example of Michael, the Arch Angel rebuking Satan. Then move on from them without attacking them back (Silence is Golden). That is one way of loving your enemy without fighting them; by not treating them the way they treat you. (Please know that God hates evil but loves all people. So, we can love the person but hate the evil in them.) Always remember that vengeance belongs to the Lord, and that vengeance will show up in the form of them reaping what they sowed. But for you (not doing evil for evil), good will come back to you. The Lord commands us to love our enemies for that very reason (Matthew 5:43–44).

[Let me qualify the above by saying this about Reciprocity (sowing and reaping.) The law of reciprocity in the universe is set by God, but God is sovereign over those laws. It means God is not subject to the laws, the laws are subject to God. Such is the spiritual law of reciprocity which means that "reaping and sowing" is automatic. That is, God doesn't lay a hand on people when they do good things or bad things. Accordingly, human nature judges itself sooner or later.

Scripture puts an aspect of reciprocity in this context: "Some men's sins go before them, some sins follow after." It means one way or another, we will reap the damage we caused that we haven't repented of. Unresolved baggage has a way of coming back into our lives that will affect our lives and the lives of others. It will come to us sooner or later. That's not just heavenly reciprocity but the evolution of life. Life has a way of either following us or catching up to us when there are important unresolved issues in our lives. Some call it coming full circle.]

✓ JOY, THE HEART'S ENTHUSIASM!

Joy isn't the same as happiness. Happiness is based on a happenstance that comes from external conditions. Joy is internal and comes from the promise of God that is unfailing. Have you ever heard the expression they are not going to steal my joy? Well, if it is stolen it will deflate your drive and take the wind out of your sails. When faced with sorrow and grief, or even depression, "yield" to the spiritual virtue of joy. It will sustain your drive amid conditions of sorrow, sadness, and grief. You may stand still for a time, but you will not regress.

✓ **PEACE, THE HEART'S QUIETNESS!**

Peace is the opposite of war and fear. But, the war (arguments and altercations) and impending troubles rage in our minds, robbing us of the peace to press forward that's needed to get through the storms of life. Fear paralyzes but peace energizes with an "unction" of the Spirit that sees us through our storms. The fruit of peace overrides the war and fear in our minds with God's promised outcome, victory. An illustration of this kind of peace can be found in Mark 4:35-41:

After leaving the massive crowd, the Lord and His Disciples sought to cross the Sea of Galilee. When they entered into a boat and launched out to sea, a storm surge (the beginning of a hurricane) arose and the waters began to break into the boat so that it appeared that the boat would sink. But the Lord, their miracle worker was asleep on a cushion in the rear of the boat. They panicked and at the same time, they frantically woke Him up and insinuated that He didn't care that they were about to die. Isn't our journey with the Lord sometimes like that when we step out on faith? Storms, in the form of troubles and problems, arise in our lives, and it feels like the Lord is asleep and those troubles and problems will overwhelm us and drown us in sorrow. Just look beyond the storm and say, "Peace, Be Still My Soul." That may sound ineffective to you, but I'm talking about asking the Lord to speak to your storms by speaking peace to our hearts where the storm is raging. As simple as it may sound, focusing on the Lord will generate peace in our hearts. *"You will keep him in perfect peace, whose mind is stayed on You, because he trusts in You."* (Isaiah 26:3).

✓ LONGSUFFERING, THE HEART'S PATIENCE!

Longsuffering is patience and is first applied to God when dealing with the constant failings and fallings of humanity. It means that God suffers or puts up with disobedience for redemption. *"The Lord is not slack concerning His promise, as some count slackness, but is longsuffering toward us, not willing that any should perish but that all should come to repentance"* (2 Peter 3:9 NKJV). Everybody seems to be in a hurry just out of habit. Therefore, patience is paramount in a hectic world to put up with the mad dash and the impulse to avoid taking shortcuts in life. But always remember, patience isn't an emotion. So, we must "yield" to the virtue of patience when needed for waiting. Patience is for "waiting" on the Lord to avoid what impatience can lead to. Just think of road rage . . . Like all the virtues of the fruit of the Spirit, practically, patience is a willful commitment to take your time with what you are doing, plan, and by no means procrastinate, regardless of the circumstances. It develops through troubled situations.

- ✓ **GENTLENESS, THE HEART'S SENSITIVITY!**

    In our world today, coming from your particular generation, I think you can see that more people today are not as sensitive to others as they used to be. May I add, they are ultra-sensitive about themselves to the degree of taking everything "personal," so one has to walk on eggshells regarding what to say or do in the presence of some people so they do not offend them. Then the conversation and activities are limited which makes the relationship awkward. It is an inversion of personality: We should be balanced emotionally between our subjectivity and objectivity about other people. Gentleness brings that balance by putting our disgruntled tendencies at arm's length where we do not take things "personal" if it isn't our heart's intent. We then become considerate of others.

- ✓ **GOODNESS, THE HEART'S GENEROUSITY!**

    Goodness stems from God's magnanimous nature and is first of all, about God's Magnanimous Giving. That is abundant forgiveness and freedom from selfishness. God's goodness and the fruit of goodness are unselfish, not resentful, or vindictive. Goodness comes from a caring heart. Goodness becomes generous when people have genuine needs and they are within our power and proximity to help them. Whether financial or resources are needed, goodness provides more than material things. It is a willingness to give, expecting nothing in return except to benefit the life or lives of the recipients. **Goodness is magnanimous giving. Magnanimous people care about the undeserved problems and troubles of others and are kind-hearted towards them.**

- ✓ **FAITH, THE HEART'S CONFIDENCE!**

    The "fruit" of faith is not the same as *"pistis"* (Saving Faith: To rely on another for salvation). The fruit of faith grows within our personalities like all the virtues. It grows from the "unction" of the Spirit. So whenever the task before us (along our journey and mission) is bigger than usual and significant to God's call upon our lives, the Spirit of God will "well up" "confidence" in our heart to push through the challenges (1 John 3:18-22).

- ✓ **MEEKNESS, THE HEART'S SUBMISSION!**

    Meekness isn't a weakness but a true strength of a humble character. It takes a bigger man or woman to walk away from an altercation when they know they can defeat their opponent. So don't confuse meekness with passivity and being non-resistant to evil. When faced with evil meekness meets and confronts the challenge. Meekness does not do "evil for evil," but will counter evil with good, and at the same time will not allow our lives to be trampled over. Meek Belivers can be aggressive when faced with challenges that stand in their way, like the Lord when he cleansed the Temple. The Lord wasn't moved by anger or rage. Rather, He was moved by righteous indignation, and so should we.

- ✓ **TEMPERANCE, THE HEART'S SELF-CONTROL!**

    Temperance is self-control and the undergirding fruit of the Spirit. It grows balance within the person's personality: the balance between the discipline to refrain from temptation and the fortitude to press forward when pursuing God's purpose. Or, as previously stated "Discipline grants us restraint from bad habits and drive for good habits for the body, mind, and soul." It implies that those skills must be practiced, or our faith must be put into practice.

Against such things there is no law.

THE FRUIT OF THE SPIRIT PRODUCES INCARNATIONAL LIVING THAT IS NOT CONDEMNED BY THE LAW OF CONSCIENCE BECAUSE LOVE ANSWERS TO A HIGHER AUTHORITY AND ADAPTS TO CIVIL LAWS IN SOCIETY! (1 Corinthians 9:19-23)

Job did not have these qualities because the Covenant Promise to be fulfilled by the Messiah had not been fulfilled. The New Covenant Promise entails the indwelling of the Spirit that would put the love of God in our hearts, thus fulfilling the law, and placing us in the "Body of Christ" as a Family (Jeremiah 31:31-34). Yet, without the enabling grace of the New Covenant, Job persevered and overcame the odds against him and was mentioned by James (the brother of the Lord) in James 5:10-11: *"As an example of suffering and patience, brothers and sisters, take the prophets who spoke in the Lord's name. Think of how we regard as blessed those who have endured. You have heard of Job's endurance and you have seen the Lord's purpose, that the Lord is full of compassion and mercy."*

HOW MUCH MORE ARE WE BLESSED UNDER THE PROVISIONS OF THE NEW COVENANT OF "GRACE" THAN THOSE WHO WERE UNDER THE DISCIPLINE OF THE LAW! (Hebrews 11:39-40).

NEXT: *God's Plan—The Way of Righteousness*

CHAPTER 8

God's Plan: The Way of Righteousness

Chapter Overview

Here, we begin with authentic Christianity compared to religious Christianity. You may scratch your head when you hear that God is not a God of religion. After 95 AD and the passing of all the Apostles, Christianity "became" (historically) an institutionalized religion. But, in all reality, the God of Scripture stands above religion and seeks to reach all people, even those in other religions. You may also be surprised and taken aback by this statement from Acts 11:26. The title Christianity did not come from heaven. It came from critics of Christianity who mocked "the followers of the Way of the Lord." So, that's what Christianity means and it comes from men ridiculing Christ's followers. But the Early Church was known as the Body of Christ: An organic movement of all ethnicities, and cultures with diverse backgrounds and economic statuses in all places at all times; with Christ as Head of His Body. The Body gathers together whenever and wherever for worship minus the element of entertainment. The Body fellowships together away from the gathering and serves each other and by reaching humanity with good news. The Body of Christ is a universal collective consciousness of people all around the world. Therefore, the preference of some is to be called disciples of the Lord. From there we proceed to unfold God's eternal plan of salvation that removes the surprise element from the path that we take toward righteousness. We then explore the way of righteousness to determine how we live by faith.

Salvation is deliverance from the penalty, power, and presence of the effects of the fall, called sin by tradition.

Religion creates robot-like followers who follow routines and rituals prescribed in their approach to God. Daily they live by rituals and routines and when those rituals and routines are not followed they become riddled with guilt and shame. To rid themselves of guilt and shame they seek God through some form of sacrifice to appease God, ward off evil, and for God to grant them good fortune.

On the other hand, authentic Christianity is free from religion and is more about a lifestyle of pleasing God in the real world, where we live, work, and play, free from guilt and shame. The Christian life isn't governed by legalistic laws. It is a life that follows the inner convictions of the heart instead of outward man-made rules and regulations. *"But if you are led by the Spirit, you are not under the law"* (Galatians 5:18).

Thus, the Path of Righteousness is about a disciple of Christ and their journey toward Christ-likeness following their "personal" convictions that come from the inner workings of God's Spirit.

Being a spiritual disciple of the Lord means that our lives are being transformed from grace to grace, strength to strength, and glory to glory as we come into the likeness of Christ-like character and virtues of the Lord. To achieve that, the Christian life isn't governed by laws (Romans 13) but by grace and love.

SPIRITUAL DISCIPLES OF THE LORD, LIKE THE LORD, ARE NOT ENGAGED IN THE DEBATABLE

THINGS OF THE WORLD AND PUBLIC OPINION. THEY ARE LASER-FOCUSED ON THE HEBREW "SHEMA" THAT FINDS ITS FULFILLMENT IN THE "GREAT COMMISSION." HOWEVER, THE THINGS OF GOD THAT THEY SHARE SHINE A LIGHT ON WHAT IS GOOD AND BEST FOR PEOPLE.

As many of you should know, the label Christian became a stigma. It was a mockery and ridicule of those who were "followers of the Way of the Lord" in Acts 11:26. That's "actually" what Christianity means in its original language. So the name Christian did not come from God. It came from religious men who blasphemed the name of the Lord. Translators took it as a badge of honor and added it as the name of the Christian Community to identify with the Lord and it subsequently became the Church. The Greek for Church is "Ecclesia," meaning a Covenant Community of Believers Called Out from under the Course of the World. Those are fundamental definitions and descriptions of the Body of Christ that we call the Church on a Mission to the World. **The Church is not a static organization but a living spiritual organism of unified Believers on the move in the world reaching all people.**

Christianity is essentially a Covenant Community in a relationship with the Mediator of the New Covenant (The Lord) and each other in the Body of Christ. So, the faith perspective of the Covenant Community should focus on the Lord and bonding relationships with those in the Body of Christ regardless of race, ethnicity, culture, background, or socio-economic status.

—*God's Plan Prepares for Surprises*—

Do you think the omniscient God was taken by surprise when Lucifer rebelled and Adam disobeyed God's Command? God's pre-ordained plan (in omniscience) considers what will happen before it happens (foreknowledge) and lays out a path of faith to follow of one's free will. Keep that thought in mind as we explore following the plan of God.

Whatever the Lord permits and allows (bad and good), there is a purpose and plan behind it to elevate our lives. When our lives are elevated (edified) by the Lord it is synonymous with "lifting up Christ" (John 12:32). The point here is when we glorify the Lord we also eliminate the surprises when we encounter and are faced with a crisis that we didn't expect or anticipate. It's like not reading the fine lines on a contract that can legally "bind" you and get you into trouble if you don't abide by it. **Let's cover the bases so there are no surprises when we encounter trouble.**

Why no surprises? God is never taken by surprise and reveals to the servants of the Lord knowledge of the Kingdom of God, and there are no surprises in the Kingdom of God. The Lord stated, *"I no longer call you slaves, because the slave does not understand what his master is doing. But I have called you friends, because I have revealed to you everything I heard from my Father"* (John 15:15). God doesn't keep us in the dark. God brings us to the light and the revelation of truth. When we are walking by faith, we are delving into the unknown that's made known by God's Spirit in us.

. . . *Things that no eye has seen, or ear heard, or mind imagined, are the things God has prepared for those who love him.*

God has revealed these to us by the Spirit. For the Spirit searches all things, even the deep things of God.

For who among men knows the things of a man except the man's spirit within him? So too, no one knows the things of God except the Spirit of God.

Now we have not received the spirit of the world, but the Spirit who is from God, so that we may know the things that are freely given to us by God.

And we speak about these things, not with words taught us by human wisdom, but with those taught by the Spirit, explaining spiritual things to spiritual people.

The unbeliever does not receive the things of the Spirit of God, for they are foolishness to him. And he cannot understand them, because they are spiritually discerned.

The one who is spiritual discerns all things, yet he himself is understood by no one.

For who has known the mind of the Lord, so as to advise him? ***But we have the mind of Christ*** (1 Corinthians 1:9-16).

Job made things right when he repented and forgave his associates which is a journey toward healing from trauma and trouble.

We heal through pain, whether spiritual, mental, emotional, or physical. Think about it . . . For that to happen, we must push through the resistance of pain. In other words, all forms of injury cause pain that we must not give in to: Don't react to your problems by getting back at those who caused the pain . . . .

—*The Way of Righteousness*—

The way of righteousness is the opposite of the way of the world in terms of direction. They are "diametrically" opposed to each other. For a Believer to go the way of the world, it would be a conflict of lifestyles. There's no straddling the fence. Either we conform to the ways of the world which will become disappointing and frustrating because a true Believer will not "fit" in and be seen as weird and ridiculed. Or they can continue along the path of righteousness living a happy, complete, fulfilled life without sinking into the activities that consume one's lifestyle. I think you know what I'm saying: There is a party atmosphere in the world today.

As stated at the beginning of this book: The "flesh," or human nature is driven to avoid pain and seek pleasure. So chasing money and spending money to look good and be "liked" consumes some people's efforts to be happy. They deify and memic the images of celebrities and erupt with pandemonia at their concerts as if they are worshipping a god. That leads to a debilitating, draining, exhausting life, filled with chaos, and confusion, ultimately ending in a dead end. It can become a drug-induced lifestyle to keep up the pace. Our hopes and dreams will be dashed!

But human existence is human existence so how can the path of righteousness be seen as any different from the way of the world? Well, I think it can be broken down in a visual.

The world—as a whole—chooses a way that is free from pain and offers extravagant living. Although that's not a reality for the vast majority of people who lack the income to make that happen, the "golden carrot" of the "American Dream" exists in the minds of most people. In most cases, the pleasures of life and luxury become visions of grandeur or an elusive pipe dream. I call it going down the rabbit hole. (You should read the Book of Ecclesiastes for some wisdom and insight on this point.)

If you know anything about that cliché about a rabbit hole, you know it means that rabbits have more than one entrance and exit to their dens. So if an animal chases the rabbit down its hole, it can escape through another hole. Or, if you shoot at a rabbit, don't expect that rabbit to come back out of the same hole. In other words, it's an elusive dream that will never happen, so let's get real about our ambitions and desires.

Following the way of the world, one can get lost in the maze of misdirection and gobbled up in the activities of the world. *"Take your share of suffering as a good soldier of Christ Jesus. No one in military service gets entangled in matters of everyday life; otherwise he will not please the one who recruited him.* (2 Timothy 2:3-4 NKJV). Following the Way of the Lord doesn't mean that we can not enjoy our lives in the real world. What it does mean is we should choose the people we associate with and the places where we go wisely.

—*How It Looks?*—

Here's How Following the Way of the Lord Looks in Society:

There is a difference between social **moral values** and **spiritual values**. Social values are based on our Judeo-Christian heritage and can range anywhere between what's in the Bible and what people think is in the Bible. Although the convictions of the heart govern a Believer's life, we are "called" by Scripture and God to abide by the laws that govern society. The difference is, if those same laws are not in a foreign culture, we do not have to keep those laws there. Nonetheless, the Moral Law known as the Ten Commandments should be kept across the board regardless of where we are.

Spiritual values are based on the attributes of God found in the fruit of the Spirit and referred to as "higher righteousness" by the Lord in Matthew 5:20. A true disciple, for the sake of furthering "Good News" will adapt to social and moral values when necessary (1 Corinthians 9:19-23).

—Following the Way of the Lord by Conviction of the Heart—

Then Jesus said to those Judeans who had believed him, "If you continue to follow my teaching, you are really my disciples and you will know the truth, and the truth will set you free' (John 8:31-32)

This is where the "human will" marries "Sovereign Will." Let me begin here with a passage of Scripture that speaks that truth loud and clear: *"If you abide in Me, and My words abide in you, you will ask what you desire, and it shall be done for you. By this My Father is glorified, that you bear much fruit; so you will be My disciples"* (John 15:7-8 NKJV).

When the human will (of its own volition) marries by submitting to God's plan and purpose, it produces a "desire" to do God's Will above all. Consequently, the prayers that are prayed focus on God's Will for the person's life and are answered because God "delights" in being pleased by the petition. So, when Scripture says, *"Delight thyself in the Lord and He will give you the desires of your heart"* (Psalms 37:4-7), it means that our desires become God's Will, like Solomons's request to judge God's people justly. **Essentially, it means to "seek first the Kingdom of God and His righteousness" and all the things we desire and need will be added.**

****

Note the immediate answer to Job's prayer when he prayed for his friends: *"When Job prayed for his friends, the LORD restored his fortunes. In fact, the LORD gave him twice as much as before! Then all his brothers, sisters, and former friends came and feasted with him in his home"* (Job 42:10-17 NLT).

Despite his self-righteousness, Job felt like he did not deserve what happened to him, and he didn't. But he still held on to his integrity and God raised his sense of righteousness to focus on the Lord of Glory through his trial. It means that when we are going through a trial God is stripping us down to bare grain so we can see that we are undeserving of the blessings of the Lord. Then grace is the only answer—God doing for us what we can't do for ourselves so none of us can declare ourselves righteous.

The essence of righteousness is making things right with God and others, and having a heartfelt reverence for God, self-respect, and respect for others. Job made things right when he repented and forgave his accusers.

NEXT: *Down the Rabbit Hole: Running From the Problem*

CHAPTER 9

Down the Rabbit Hole: Running From the Problem

Chapter Overview

If you are dreaming the impossible dream and chasing the elusive golden carrot of the American Dream, you are headed down a rabbit hole. Essentially, the expression means looking for something or someone that you will never find. Here, we look at ourselves and the trauma, troubles, and problems that hurt us and send us into fight or flight. We begin by looking at the heritage of trauma and pain that we inherited from the first humans.

Down the rabbit hole is an English language idiom, cliché, or a common everyday expression. It is a metaphoric-ironic saying about getting in too deep into something and ending up somewhere unexpected. It derives from the expression of a rabbit running to escape capture either by a hunter or another predator. If a rabbit is being hunted or chased and they happen to reach their hole in time, more than likely, what was chasing them or hunting them will lose them. They will lose them because there is more than one hole to a rabbit's den. So, they can go down one hole and escape out of another. **If you are dreaming the impossible dream and chasing the elusive golden carrot, you are headed down a rabbit hole.**

The question is, "What are we looking for in life or what are we running from?" In this case, humanly speaking, we tend to run from something looking for something else. The irony is that when we run from our problems, looking for a way out, we will run dab-smack into the same problem when we look in the mirror. **So, let's look at us and the trauma, troubles, and problems that hurt us and send us into fight or flight.** Let's begin by taking our pain out of the personal category and look at the problem objectively concerning the origin of trauma and pain with the first humans.

Down the rabbit hole takes us on a journey of running from a problem of human nature failures without the help of God.

Here, the Rabbit Hole is also about looking for love in all the wrong places. I don't need to name-drop those places and people because they speak for themselves when we encounter disappointment. But those places and people can be identified by the idea of looking for meaning in life in meaningless ways. So, what are we clamoring about? LOVE! The most wicked man and woman in the world wants to be loved. It is a testament to love as the most powerful force. Well, why not try loving God and yourself to see what it produces in your quest for love instead of running down a rabbit hole?

The Heritage of Trauma and Pain

Our trauma and pain aren't unique to us, but a malady of humanity that began with one man and one woman, if you believe the Creation Story and the Genesis Saga. A good way to help calm the mental and emotional anguish of trauma and trouble is taken from 1 Corinthians 10:13. *"No trial has overtaken you that is not faced by others. And God is faithful: He will not let you be tried beyond what you are able to bear, but with the trial will also provide a way out so that you may be able to endure it."* We should muse on those thoughts. The providence of trouble also enables us to effectively minister to others because of what we've gone through.

Blessed is the God and Father of our Lord Jesus Christ, the Father of mercies and God of all comfort,

who comforts us in all our troubles so that we may be able to comfort those experiencing any trouble with the comfort with which we ourselves are comforted by God.

For just as the sufferings of Christ overflow toward us, so also our comfort through Christ overflows to you (2 Corinthians 1:3-5).

Knowing that others are experiencing similar problems and pain has a way of putting our ailments somewhat at ease in the Big Picture of life. So here's the Big Picture of how all our troubles and problems originated and the solution.

****

Why did mankind yield to the temptation of the woman to disobey God? Most of us do not consider the human elements behind his decision because we only see the surface of the man recorded in Scripture. But human nature is human nature regardless of the generation. Although they lived in antiquity and we live in modernity, they had similar problems as we have today in their thinking, behavior, and relationships. We don't consider the first man or his descendants' *emotions*, *intellect*, and *will* because we see them as pristine personalities beyond reproach, or like fictitious characters. So, how were his inner workings involved in his failures and the ensuing fall? It was the fall of man that opened (so-to-speak) the

Pandora's Box of all sin, suffering, sickness, and disease. Let's postulate:

Adam was fully human in his constitution, minus the propensity to disobey God—the sin gene he and his posterity inherited after the fall. Some theology says that he was created in innocence. Innocence at the inception of creation was about ignorance of good or evil. (Keep that thought in mind as we move on.) For a moment, consider this common sense "take" on the first humans being created in innocence:

People are not born good or evil, which makes them neutral concerning doing good or evil. That's what made the first man and woman innocent. The difference between their innocence and our innocence is they were ignorant of good or evil, but we are not. Their awareness of good and evil entered the human constitution after the fall in the form of guilt and shame. Environmentally, through nurture, we learn to be good or evil. So if he didn't have the propensity to disobey God, why did he?

Unquestionably, he was created to procreate humanity (*"Be Fruitful And Multiply And Replenish The Earth"*). Thus, Adam means humankind. Consequently, in physiology, he was given the biological capacity to begat children with his wife who was created from his side. (She was his equal with a different role and responsibility.) So his human sexuality wasn't a sin.

To fulfill the command of God to procreate humanity, he was also given the biological sex hormone testosterone to regulate his libido for sex drive and his wife was likewise given estrogen for sexual pleasure. This is why sex (although pleasurable for procreation) is sacred in the Eyes of God and confined to marriage for the sake of family. But, let's face it, failed marriages and broken relationships abound and are a huge reality in our world. But there is a remedy for a fresh start if you experience failure or brokenness in a relationship: repentance, forgiveness, and moving on. **In**

any case, it's called the road to recovery. Although we don't know the duration of Job's trial, all the maladies of common human nature were part of his crisis and he was restored. So, let's do an analysis of human nature involved with his disobedience leading to his recovery.

****

The root meaning of sin in Hebrew and Greek is a "Trespass" or "Transgression": To violate the revealed Will of God. (We have looked at this before, but here, we are looking at it with the first humans.) Note again the revealed Will of God, meaning that just because it is recorded in Scripture it doesn't mean that God has revealed "our" sin to our hearts.

Because of free will, one must become aware and convicted that what they are doing is a sin. That's the main point behind the Lord's admonition about hearing the "Good News" of salvation and redemption in His Words recorded in Matthew 24:14 about our inner witness, the human conscience. If the Gospel of the Kingdom of God witnesses to a person's heart that Jesus is indeed Lord, and they reject it, it becomes unpardonable. For it to be pardoned, it must be forgiven, and to be forgiven, the person must repent. If they do not repent, the witness of their conscience will bear witness against them. That's what I mean, we judge ourselves by our conscience.

"And this gospel of the kingdom shall be preached in all the world for a witness unto all nations; and then shall the end come" (Matthew 24:14 KJV). Note again "witness," meaning that their conscience becomes their inner witness to the truth and makes them accountable.

****

Concerning God being a Just God and God's Judicial System of Divine Justice, it means before a person can be charged for disobeying God, God must reveal it to the person's heart. A natural analogy is when we are subpoenaed to a court of law as a witness to a crime. If we don't appear as a witness we will be charged with contempt of court resulting in a fine. In God's court, we too are fined and penalized for disobeying our inner witness to the Truth. The difference is we judge ourselves.

That's the difference between man's system of justice and God's. God's justice is what God declares as just and right based on how God sees human nature. It comes from God revealing to our hearts Yeshua as the Messiah and the act of Him paying for our penalty with His "own" life as our vicarious sufferer. When we believe in Him, we are declared righteous and set free from the penalty and punishment of sin and death because the Lord took our place.

When God guides us into the Will of God, the Spirit of God prods our hearts as conviction. If we disobey God's voice from the heart, that's when it becomes a sin. It means that Adam wasn't ignorant of God's Will and intentionally (Willfully-1 Timothy 2:14) disobeyed, but why? Let's look at it from a pragmatic biological standpoint; not the typical theological perspective. But, hold your horses, the result can be the same.

Here the means doesn't justify the end or the end the means. What matters is what his disobedience resulted in and that is the fall of humankind away from God.

****

A synonym for sin is also to "err": To go astray and wander off the path of righteousness. Thus, the word "error" means to make a mistake in judgment and fall short of God's revealed Will. These definitions are a long way to saying that Adam made a "mistake" or an error in judgment. Then what was his error in judgment? First, he wasn't deceived or confused (1 Timothy 2:14). Second, to fully understand it, we must look at it in the converse, meaning that if we could experience the consequences of our sin that gets us in trouble before we commit the act, we would never commit the act. That's a mistake or an error in judgment because we don't fully know the consequences.

No one is a glutton for punishment unless they are caught up in the erroneous doctrine of asceticism or have developed a perversion of nature. So, here, Adam made a mistake and erred in his judgment. I believe that he may have thought that he would lose his wife to death and rather than lose her, he decided to share her fate. But, a closer analysis of Scripture indicates that the penalty of death was on his head and not his wife's. So, in theory, he miscalculated and if he refused to give in to the temptation driven by their copulation and sexual pleasure, he could have redeemed her, stayed where he was, and prevented the fall. That's a pragmatic story behind the fall of man. As unbiblical as it may sound to the self-righteous, you could say he fell because of sex. Ever since then, great men in Scripture and throughout history have fallen for the same reason.

I know some of you are finding this hard to believe because we deify biblical characters and become so heavenly-minded that we are no earthly good. But from our secular-carnal real-world mindsets, we perceive biblical characters as highly moral people. But what verifies the authenticity of Scripture as a divinely inspired work is the fact that if it were penned merely by men, the flaws and shortcomings of the great characters, known as sin would have been covered up, but they aren't.

Great characters in the Bible did some wrong things common to human nature, like Noah and his drunkenness, Abraham and his lying, and David and his adultery and murder. Should I go on with other characters? But bear with me for a moment to say this in finality:

People throughout Scripture and history are no different from people today except for technological advances of modernity. Human nature is human nature throughout time and doesn't appear to be getting any better as claimed by social evolutionists. They say, that as we climb the moral ladder and get better based on the quality of life, and life expectancy, implying that human nature is "basically" good. Human nature isn't "basically" evil and neither is it "basically" good. If that were true, we would see more good in the world. What makes us good is a Good God and what makes us evil is destructive choices.

****

Let me digress: Why did Adam, meaning humanity, allow himself to be seduced into disobeying the command of God that forbade him to eat from the Tree of Knowledge of Good and Evil? And why a tree? I believe the tree was literal and the effects of eating were real too, but not in terms of the fruit having a debilitating or remedial effect. **The capacity for good and evil was already in the soul through the power of choice to obey or disobey.** Obeying would lead to a life beyond our imagination because we don't know. But, let me say this for what it is worth.

As stated in chapter three, in Genesis 1:1 and 1:2, God separated time from eternity. **The fact that God separated time from eternity before the first humans were created is an indication that they were mortal beings upon creation.** Nonetheless, even after the fall, the chronology and genealogy of the male posterity lived well into hundreds of years. Methuselah lived to be 969 years old (Genesis 5:27), and was considered the longest-living human being. So, how long would humanity have lived if Adam had not disobeyed God? I don't know and your guess is as good as mine, but they would have had very long lives. And, after death, all human beings (because sin would not be in the human constitution) would go through the portal of death without dying like Enoch, who walked with God and was translated. Translated to what can be surmised as eternal life or immortality. After all, only God can create immortality. I don't think Science will ever figure that one out because the soul is immortal, not the body. Immortality is a gift of eternal life, after death.

  We know that his disobedience opened ("so to speak") a pandora's box and every evil known to humankind was unleashed on him, his wife, his children, and his posterity. That is right down to our generation and the child being born right now. What translations merely state is he sinned, but a closer examination of human nature can produce a deductive answer concerning "why."

****

My objective regarding life-long ministry is to help people become better human beings by embracing their humanity. I know that may seem contrary to traditional Christian thought because human nature is deemed sinful by those indoctrinated into the sin syndrome of dual natures (soul and body). However, a closer look at Scripture reveals that humankind was created in the image of God (imago dei—Genesis 1:26-27), and the fall of man defaced and marred that image, but it is restored in redemption.

Coming up in the Conclusion, I will introduce the "Human Condition" and the "Faith Condition" which identify how and why people fall and are redeemed.

As far as my research has taken me, most religions, regardless of the distinctives, focus primarily on the divine through theology, doctrine, and dogma, to find God, reach God, and worship God through ceremonies, rituals, and routine customs to appease God and ward off evil and guarantee good fortune. That's a mouthful!

The perspective of faith in the Lord of Glory isn't to appease God for protection against evil and good fortune. It is love for the Lord because of His redeeming love. *"We love him, because he first loved us"* (1 John 4:19). My point is we know much more about the Lord's divinity than we know about His humanity. As generalized as it sounds, the point I make in the previous statements is a verifiable conception of religion as a whole, even among the various Christian denominations and local church affiliations. We see that clearly through the life of Job. He followed rituals (early forms of sacrifice) and routines to worship and serve God. **However, seldom do we hear about the role of human nature in congruence with the divine. To grasp that, we should have a basic understanding of human nature in its quest to serve and please God.**

Let's take a look at human frailty, imperfections, and the mistakes we are "subject" to make by our choices due to the inherited nature to disobey God that we were born with. The most serious conflict between human fate and divine destiny takes place between what translations describe as *"flesh and Spirit."* Note on the diagram in the concluding chapter that the "flesh" can be seen as the soul expressed through the body or the vehicle of the expression of the heart. Although Spirit is in the upper case indicating the Spirit of God, God's Spirit occupies the human spirit upon regeneration, referred to as "the new birth." Again, that's my faith perspective and it may not be yours.

You can consider the points here after viewing the diagram. But based on your reflections from the diagram, I'd like to share my pragmatic views on the flaws, frailties, mistakes, and errors in judgment that lead to wrong decisions called "sin" by misapplied doctrine. Then we assume that a sinner is a bad person, when in fact, under the dispensation of grace, a believer is no longer described as a sinner in status before the Lord of Glory but as a "son and daughter of God" through justification. Take a look at the diagram in the concluding chapter and let's break down the meaning.

The intricacies linguistically from both the Hebrew and Greek words for sin means to fail at fulfilling God's Will because human nature is born out of communion with God due to the fall. Thus, the term "sinner" applies only to the unregenerate, those alienated from the life of God.

Concerning the fall of humanity before salvation offered by the Lord of Glory, all humanity fell short of God's salvation by faith (Romans 3:23). The reason stated for failing is the state of the unregenerate or a person who hasn't experienced the new birth offered to those who believe in the Lord. I'm not countering anyone's view of a relationship with God. I'm just stating mine. So, believers in the Lord are not sinners or bad people, even though they may sin from time to time. Now, let's look at the rest of the story . . . .

NEXT: The Conclusion—The Problem (The Human Condition)-The Solution (The Faith Condition)

CONCLUSION

The Human Condition versus The Faith Condition

Chapter Overview

We begin with a genetic analysis of spiritual DNA within human DNA. The theological concept of Original Sin was developed by St. Augustine, Bishop of Hippo in North Africa, and one of the Fathers of the Roman Catholic Church around 354 and 430 AD. I address this piece of Church History because it occurred around the same time Scripture was canonized into 66 Books inspired by God. It all happened before the copied text of Scripture was translated which means the thoughts of Augustine were incorporated into the King James translation. My question is, were Augustine's thoughts inspired by God too? Here I will elaborate on Original Sin and unravel the condemnation associated with the mistakes people make that religious-minded people call sin. **Consequently, we will look at how spiritual separation affects three forms of human separation: Positive Separation; Negative Separation, and Toxic Separation. Spiritual union restores relationships.** The diagrams disclosed here will give you a visual of the information.

—*Spiritual DNA within Natural DNA*—

Genetics can be a difficult science to understand. Each human being has twenty-three pairs of chromosomes. Twenty-three come from the male (father) and twenty-three come from the female (mother) for a total of 46 in each offspring. Each of these forty-six chromosomes carries *information (DNA)* that determines physical characteristics, such as complexion, eye color, hair texture, hair color, height, etc. **Those are outer physical characteristics.**

In some cases, depending on *heritage, environmental conditions, biological transference,* **inner personality traits**, and **habits** can also be transmitted. This means that we can inherit some of the *inner character traits* and *habits* of our parents. That inheritance comes from biological heritage and the theological concept of original sin. But first, let me add an editorial about Original Sin:

[The theological concept of Original Sin was developed by St. Augustine, Bishop of Hippo in North Africa. He was also one of the Fathers of the Roman Catholic Church. His classical thoughts contributed to Orthodox and Latin Christianity. He wrote extensively on the Trinity and the human condition reflected in the soul of man. Thus, his theological concept of Original Sin was fully developed between 354 and 430 AD, following his conversion to Christianity. In Latin, original sin was called *"peccatum originale."* Note here that he wrote his work as a rebuttal of Pelagius's controversial theology about free will. Pelagius espoused that all humans have God-given free will and choose to obey God's commands. Therefore he saw sin as a choice instead of a propensity inherited from Adam. He also believed that human beings can live a sinless life if that's their choice. However, Augustine was orthodox in his thinking and added his "own" thinking about the Trinity which is also reflected in the human soul and Original Sin. I think you can see

why I'm addressing this piece of Church History. The reason is the Canonization of Scripture occurred around the same time. The 66 Books of the Bible that were considered inspired by God were completed (Including Augustine's thoughts about the Trinity and Original Sin). My point is, that it all happened before the copied text of Scripture was translated, therefore also incorporated into the King James translation.]

Original Sin & The Propensity Gene

Considering the above editorial, I hold to the fundamentals of Original Sin and dismiss Pelagius's argument. However, the thoughts of Augustine were incorporated into the King James translation. **My question is, were Augustine's thoughts also inspired by God?** Here I will elaborate on the concept of Original Sin disclosed from the original languages of Scripture before Scripture was translated.

Romans 5:12, 14: *"Therefore, just as sin entered the world through one man, and death through sin, and in this way death came to all people, because all sinned...Nevertheless, death reigned from the time of Adam to the time of Moses, even over those who did not sin by breaking a command, as did Adam, who is a pattern of the one to come"* (NIV).

Adam's transgression led to the penalty of death for all humanity. If we have eyes to see, the penalty of death opened a door to the gift of eternal life and initiated the process of salvation and redemption. It gave God the advantage and edge to build the expanded Kingdom of God through the free will of those who would receive the Lord. Without the penalty of death, there would be no salvation. God demonstrated the work of redemption that would be wrought by the "Seed" of the woman in Genesis 3:15, *"And I will put hostility between you and the woman and between your offspring and her offspring, he will strike your head, and you will strike his heel."*

In the text above, the Lord utters the "Good News" of redemption in time setting the stage for the Messiah to come down through 42 generations in fulfillment of the Lord's prophetic words. Galatians 4:4-5, *"But when the set time had fully come, God sent his Son, born of a woman, born under the law, to redeem those under the law, that we might receive adoption to sonship."* Genesis 3:15 was precise because Satan, that old serpent, bruised the heel of the Lord when He went to Golgatha and gave His life for our lives. But when He gave His life, He bruised the head of the serpent. That is, Christ's work on Calvary destroyed the hold that Satan had over humanity through the penalty of **death** because He paid the penalty with His life, death, and resurrection.

****

Death can be defined with one word, **SEPARATION.** First, there is **physical death** (The separation of the soul from the body). Second, there is **spiritual death** (The separation of the soul from God). Then there is **eternal death** (Eternal banishment and separation of consciousness from God's presence due to willful rejection of the Lord.). Humanly speaking, that may sound cruel for a loving God, but keep in mind we judge ourselves.

Every person alive throughout history will be allowed to acknowledge the Lord as Savior, but everyone will not believe, even with evidence. I draw this conclusion by connecting the dots of Scripture correlated with the corruption of human nature throughout history. You probably don't believe this because of what you have heard from various pulpits, but if they fail to acknowledge the Lord before they die, they will have another opportunity to acknowledge the Lord at the White Throne Judgment. Even with evidence before them, some will still refuse because evil knows no repentance. But the question remains, "Where does the soul go after death?" If the soul is imperishable as many contend, the soul will not go into oblivion and cease to exist. Instead, our consciousness will live on somewhere in the universe. The question is where? Or, is there no hell or heaven?

In Milton's "Paradise Lost," he tells the Hollywood fictitious version of hell. His story is drawn from several passages of Scripture about Lucifer's rebellion against God. The famous quote that comes from the epic story is, "Better to reign in Hell than serve in Heaven." It makes a point about fallen humanity too. Rather than serve God and God's people, I believe that Satan's lie will be so effective that some will think they can have free reign in hell.

Spiritual separation affects three forms of human separation in relationships: **Positive Separation** when people leave each other on a friendly basis; **Negative Separation** when people leave each other on an unfriendly basis due to some form of abuse, or abandonment. Although cumulative in effect, it usually happens suddenly leaving the person surprised. Take for example divorce. Then there is **Toxic Separation** when people leave each other because the relationship is poisonous. Negative and toxic separation causes mental/emotional pain that can linger like a scar on the soul. **Both result in arrested development.**

Concerning the first two relationships, we can leave the proverbial light on and the door open in case they want to come back into our lives. Concerning the latter, toxic relationships, the light should be turned off and the door shut. Why? Toxic relationships tend to worsen over time which means the person has to prove that they have changed over a lengthy period. Toxic relationships break hearts and a heart can only be restored by our Spiritual Physician, the Lord.

Spiritual union restores relationships. The greatest bond in a relationship is spiritual because it is the glue that holds it together. Pardon the comparison but Christ is the glue and that glue is called "agape" love.

****

Natural Headship of Adam means, "The individual receives the physical nature and soul from the parents. Thus, all people were present in Adam in germinal or seminal form (relating to *seed* or *semen*). Each individual, therefore receives Adam's propensity to disobey God because of *Federal Headship*: Adam being humanity's representative before God. **In summary, all human beings have Adam's <u>*propensity*</u>—we are all subject to disobey God at any time.**

When we consider the tenets of Original Sin, which is the passing on of Adam's transgression to the entire human race, I believe that *spiritual sin* passes on genetically, just as some diseases, and other traits. Let me explain from the perspective of the *First Man Adam* and the *Second Man Adam, Jesus Christ.*

The first Adam, the *Federal Head* of the human race passed sin on to every person born after him through his disobedience. The Second Adam, Jesus Christ, through His obedience at Calvary, passed righteousness on to everyone who believes in Him because He breaks generational curses. ***Galatians 3:13-14, "Christ redeemed us from the curse of the law by becoming a curse for us, for it is written: 'Cursed is everyone who is hung on a pole." "He redeemed us in order that the blessing given to Abraham might come to the Gentiles through Christ Jesus, so that by faith we might receive the promise of the Spirit"* (NIV).**

Our Lord Jesus Christ was sinless. He didn't inherit Adam's sin gene in His humanity because His Father was God Almighty—the incarnation of deity. Therefore, it appears in the context of male-female copulation that the sin gene is passed on by the male gender, just as the male determines the sex of the child. (We can become like our fathers without knowing them.)

According to the sacred text of Scripture, Joseph wasn't the biological father of Christ. He was conceived by insemination of the Spirit of God, thus breaking the transmission of the sin gene. Adam's propensity means that we are all subject to disobeying God at any time because the sin gene is passed on to us. However, Christ breaks the heritage of sin and death through faith.

How Christ Breaks the Heritage of Sin!

Concerning the *image of God* in man (The *Imago Dei*), God's image has been marred but not erased. The inner human constitution of man is the *still small voice of God* in his conscious testifying to the fact that man is not his own master, but responsible for a moral law that either reproves or approves. ***Romans 2:14-15, "(Indeed, when Gentiles, who do not have the law, do by nature things required by the law, they are a law for themselves, even though they do not have the law." "They show that the requirements of the law are written on their hearts, their consciences also bearing witness, and their thoughts sometimes accusing them and at other times even defending them"(NIV).***

Depending on their *faith system*, some believers hold to a **Dichotomy** (twofold nature—soul, and body.) view of the human constitution. Others hold to a **Trichotomy** (threefold nature—spirit, soul, body) view of the human constitution. My preference is the *Trichotomy* because of the nature of God in Creation.

As we continue to explore the *human condition* keep in mind that the struggle and problem of following the ways of the Lord as a disciple is within us called human nature.

THE HUMAN CONDITION

DIAGRAM OF THE IMAGE OF GOD IN MAN

Begin noting here that the soul (Self-Consciousness) is suppressed and separated from God due to the fall of man.

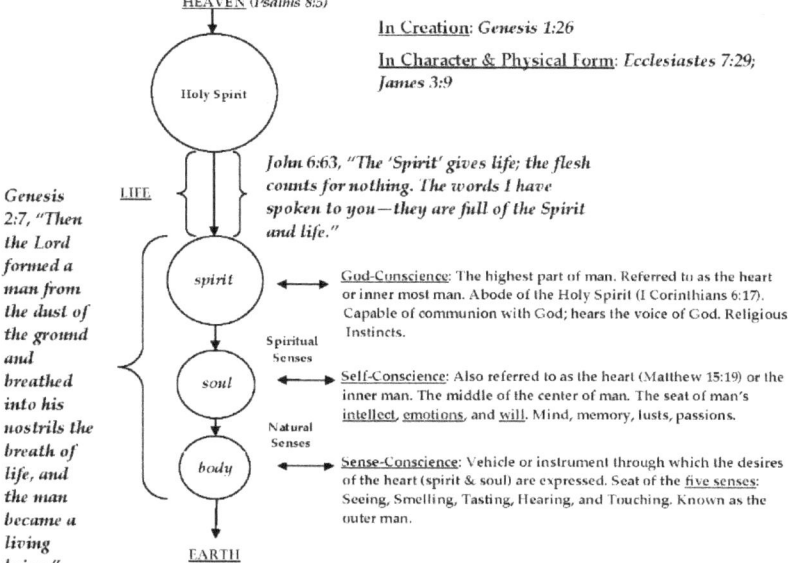

THE THREEFOLD NATURE OF MAN

I Thessalonians 5:23
May God himself, the God of peace, sanctify you through and through. May your whole spirit, soul and body be kept blameless at the coming of our Lord Jesus Christ.

Hebrews 4:12
For the word of God is alive and active. Sharper than any double-edged sword, it penetrates even to dividing soul and spirit, joints and marrow; it judges the thoughts and attitudes of the heart.

HEAVEN (Psalms 8:5)

In Creation: Genesis 1:26

In Character & Physical Form: Ecclesiastes 7:29; James 3:9

Holy Spirit

Genesis 2:7, "Then the Lord formed a man from the dust of the ground and breathed into his nostrils the breath of life, and the man became a living being."

LIFE

John 6:63, "The 'Spirit' gives life; the flesh counts for nothing. The words I have spoken to you—they are full of the Spirit and life."

spirit — God-Conscience: The highest part of man. Referred to as the heart or inner most man. Abode of the Holy Spirit (I Corinthians 6:17). Capable of communion with God; hears the voice of God. Religious Instincts.

Spiritual Senses

soul — Self-Conscience: Also referred to as the heart (Matthew 15:19) or the inner man. The middle of the center of man. The seat of man's intellect, emotions, and will. Mind, memory, lusts, passions.

Natural Senses

body — Sense-Conscience: Vehicle or instrument through which the desires of the heart (spirit & soul) are expressed. Seat of the five senses: Seeing, Smelling, Tasting, Hearing, and Touching. Known as the outer man.

EARTH

Spiritual Nature { Spirit *"Pnema"*: A blast of air, breath. } The difference is the intensity of breath.
{ Soul *"Psuche"*: To breath gently, breathe. }

Human Nature { Body *"Soma"*: The body as a sound whole. The physical instrument of life.
{ Flesh *"Sarx"*: By implication human nature. The workings of the soul and body. All physical and moral frailties and carnal passions.

Explanation of the Diagram Concerning Sin & Salvation

Here's an "exegeted" theory, so take it for what it's worth. I call it revelation knowledge by comparison of Scripture. God commanded Adam in *Genesis 2:16-17, "And the LORD God commanded the man, "You are free to eat from any tree in the garden;" " but you must not eat from the tree of the knowledge of good and evil, for when you eat from it you will certainly die."* He died physically later (*Genesis 5:3*). However, according to *man's fall*, he died spiritually and instantly on the spot. His eyes were immediately opened and he became aware of his sin (*Genesis 3:7*). Their consciousness was riddled with *guilt* and *shame*. Here's some insight into what I think happened based on the diagram.

When Adam disobeyed God, his *spirit* (God-Consciousness) fell away from God to the level of his *soul* (*Self-Consciousness*), and his God-Consciousness no longer dominated his soul, but his soul now governed his human nature. (See the Diagram) **Thus the Fall of Man! His total being became separated from God.** Not only the fellowship was lost, but the relationship between God and man was severed and Adam was alienated from the life of God, symbolically gestured by him cast out of the Garden and an Angel barring the way (*Genesis 3:23-24*).

When a believer comes to Christ as Savior, the Holy Spirit *indwells* and *quickenes* (brings to life) the human spirit. *Ephesians 2: 4-5, "But because of his great love for us, God, who is rich in mercy," "made us alive (KJV-"Quicken") with Christ even when we were dead in transgressions—it is by grace you have been saved."*

The human spirit is then radically separated from the soul (Hebrews 4:12) and the Holy Spirit makes our spirit, soul, and body God's Temple. God now lives within the human spirit (The part that communes with God and hears the voice of God). The relationship is restored (*John 1:12*) and man enters into fellowship with God. That single act is called the *indwelling of the Holy Spirit* and is the fulfillment of God's Covenant Promise. In *John 3:1-8* Christ referred to it as the *"born again"* experience or being *"born from above."* His analogy of being *"born of water"* (The breaking of the woman's water in childbirth.) points out that it is not enough to be born naturally to enter the *Kingdom of Heaven*! Point: religion won't get you into heaven without a relationship with God! We must have a second birth, born from above by God's Spirit.

****

Christ's parables were natural stories with spiritual meanings so the natural mind could comprehend the teachings. So natural birth represents spiritual birth, just as copulation in marriage is a type of intimacy between Christ and His Church. Just as the male gender (the father) *"begot"* the child, so our *Heavenly Father* begets His children. It is the man's *seed* (Greek *"Sperma"* translated into sperm) that fertilizes the woman's egg cell to conceive. It is God's Seed (The Word and Spirit—the nature of God) that enables the believer to be *born again.* **Romans 8:15-16, "The Spirit you received does not make you slaves, so that you live in fear again; rather, the Spirit you received brought about your adoption to sonship. And by him we cry, "Abba, Father." <u>The Spirit himself testifies</u> <u>with our spirit that we are God's children.</u>"**

In *1 John 3:9*, we clearly see the meaning of God's *seed* in us. ***"No one who is <u>born of God</u> will continue to sin, because God's <u>seed</u> remains in them; they cannot go on sinning, because they have been born of God."*** In practical explanation, compared to similar scriptures, it means that although they may fall into sin for a time or season, they will not continue practicing a sinful lifestyle, but will repent and get back on track.

The word *seed* there in Greek is ***"sperma"*** and implies ***offspring***. Peter pronounces in *1 Peter 1:23*, ***"For you have been born again, not of perishable seed, but of imperishable, through the living and enduring word of God."*** **HALLELUIAH!** Because of God's *seed* in the Christian, every believer will continue in their walk of faith with Christ until He comes. **They may continue to struggle with the frailties and weaknesses of their human nature; biased and subjectively perceived as sin by religious Christians. But the Holy Spirit will continue working with them in their walk of faith away from the church.** They will continue to have a relationship with God. The question for the Christian community is, "How do we restore them to fellowship."

Now let's look at the "Faith Condition" as the best solution:

THE FAITH CONDITION

I have discovered from interviews, research, exposure, Scripture, and experience that some Christians are leaving churches unannounced and attendance is declining because their faith is being challenged. After all, the core of their "personal" convictions (the heart of their spirituality) is being challenged in the wrong way.

"Spirituality is about our identity with Christ!"
"We have an individualized walk of faith within the

collective community of faith and no two believers are at the same place in their progression toward Christlikeness."

The new nature's spiritual DNA is identical to Christ and every believer has the identical Christ-like DNA. However, we retain our human DNA (human nature), which is what makes us different and Christ the Holy Spirit works uniquely with each Christian to bring them into conformity to the image of Christ IN THEIR WALK OF FAITH!

Faith is not in your Talk but in your Walk!

Some of us today are like the Pharisees in Christ's day. We are full of "hot air," without any substance or reality to our talk. We talk all theory without reality. *"For in the gospel the righteousness of God is revealed— a righteousness that is by faith from first to last, just as it is written":* ***"The righteous will live by faith"*** *(Romans 1:17-18).*

Faith is primarily for living a life that is pleasing to the Lord. Hebrews 11:6a, *"And without faith it is impossible to please God…"* Unlike what Heralders of the prosperity gospel proclaim, faith is not merely for "getting" things from God. *Matthew 6:33, "But seek first his kingdom and his righteousness, and all these things will be given to you as well."* **Getting things from God is a reward for living a pleasing life by grace.**

A good formula for faith and lifestyle is, "Where there is faith, there is Christ, where there is Christ, there is life, where there is life, there is lifestyle." Genuine biblical saving faith will eventually produce *a lifestyle* as a disciple of Jesus Christ, which is the basic fruit of the Christian life. God's Covenant Promise to every Christian is *eternal life* and *abundant life.* **Eternal life begins with the *new birth* and is actualized at** death or upon the return of Christ. Abundant life is a transformed life in the here and now.

The Greek language for *abundant* life in *John 10:10* is a reference to growth as we abide in the Vine, Christ. **Growth begins with character development—** *the fruit of the Spirit,* **and extends to reproduction on the Vine—others coming to Christ. (See John 15:1-8) The immediate benefit of salvation upon the inception of the Christian life is** *abundant life,* **which begins with a change in one's lifestyle— how we live for Christ!** However, a Christian's lifestyle is a gradual "work in progress" throughout their life. Scripture indicates throughout that no one **arrives** until Christ comes! In the interim, individual Christians cannot judge other Christians because they are not at their level of growth (*Romans 14:1-13*).

Herein lies the problem. The Westernized Church world makes a dreaded mistake when they attack and judge the sins of allied Christians in the real world by assaulting their behavior, which becomes an insult to their character. **The problem is not the human condition, but the condition of their faith.** They are in Christ with doubts and uncertainty. Correct their faith and the behavior will follow!

> *A growing number of people are leaving the institutionalized church for a new reason. They are not leaving because they have lost faith. They are leaving the church to preserve their faith. These are strong words. Could it be that the "churched culture" indeed is spiritually toxic? We have a problem?* **(Cole Neil, Organic Church-Growing Faith Where Life Happens, 2005, p. xxiii)**

As stated, they are leaving churches unannounced and attendance is declining because their faith is being challenged in the wrong way. Preachers challenge their faith to conform to a kind of dogma (A strict belief other than faith in the finished work of Christ on Calvary that insinuates a person is not saved if they do not believe what they teach.). Their teaching separates them from participation in the real world. It leaves them on a dysfunctional "guilt trip" constantly trying to figure out what they can or cannot do. In their thinking, God confines them to the four walls and campus of the church, which conflicts with a normal life (Barring the violation of the Moral Law.) where they live, work, and play. **However, how to live within Christian liberty is not taught.** Instead, teachings are about attending church, giving money to the church, and participating in the activities of the church. All of that would be okay if there was also an emphasis on the liberty of Christians living in the real world. To illustrate this point I have created a diagram (coming up) describing the **church worldview** of God versus the **real worldview** of God. But first, the following:

The Sunday Go-To-Meeting Concept

The idea of the "church world" comes from the concept of the "Sunday-go-to-meeting."

What is the Sunday-go-to-meeting concept of God? It is the sub-conscious theological notion and traditional ideology that God confines within space. Particularly, God confines within the space where worshippers meet.

I remember during my second pastorate we razed the old church building that sat adjacent to the new building to make way for more parking space. Large crowds of former and current church members gathered as the building was about to come down. They were weeping and mourning as if a human being had died and gathered bricks from the remains to memorialize the Holy Spirit in that place.

We see a classic Biblical example of that ideology in *John 4* when the racially religiously mixed Samaritan woman asked Christ a non-rhetorical question: *"Our ancestors worshiped on this mountain, but you Jews claim that the place where we must worship is in Jerusalem" (John 4:20)*. The Jews confined God to their culture because of the perception of the Covenant Promise. She wanted to know if she could remain in her culture and village and worship God, and Christ's answer was an emphatic "YES." *John 4:24, "God is spirit, and his worshipers must worship in the Spirit and in truth."*

As stated, the Samaritan woman's inquiry pointed to the Jews isolating God within the space of their culture because of the Covenant Promise. That's also the perception of real-world Christians. Although God is seeking to establish His presence on the earth through His Covenant Community (The Church), God is active in the real world (The Sphere of His Operations-*Matthew 28:18-20*). From the outside looking in, it appears as though the church world confines God to their world! The reality of Christ dulls by the Sunday-go-to-meeting concept, which means people on the outside cannot see Him "clearly." To Worship Him Dearly We Must See Him Clearly.

The Gospel of the Kingdom of God

The ***gospel of the kingdom of God*** focuses on a personal relationship with God through Jesus Christ where we live, work, play, and witness. Some church members know about God and Christ but do not have a personal relationship with Him. **They have religion without a relationship!** They have heard the various versions of the denominational gospel, but do not know the *gospel of the kingdom of God*.

The gospel of the kingdom of God in the context of the world highlights God living where the residents live. However, some believe in a subconscious way that God lives behind the four walls of the church and doesn't live where they live. Due to quasi-righteousness and holiness projected from the church world, they think their lives are not good enough for God to live where they live. Therefore, they concentrate on attendance and good works in the church world, but after the benediction, they divorce Christ from where they live in the real world! Note the diagram and description of the Church World.

ILLUSTRATION OF REAL WORLD & CHURCH WORLD FAITH VIEW

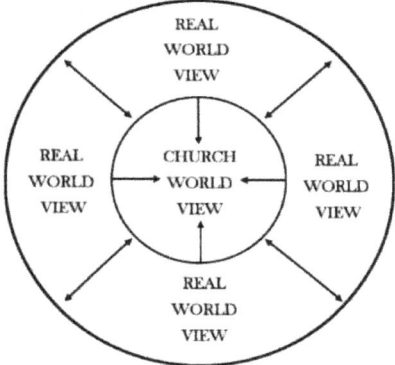

Explanation of Illustration

Explanation of Illustration: The church world tends to view the <u>presence</u> of God within the church world and see His work through a small worldview. Christians in the real world tend to see God at work in the church world and the real world where they live, work, and play. Actually, God is in both worlds at the same time! Although most Christians have an idea of the Omnipresence of God, they relegate God's presence through religious language like "anointing" and reserve God's presence to a feeling located within their church. Those who are Reformed and Conservative in their thinking relegate His presence to Knowledge based on their theological traditions. When seekers and the unchurched inquire about the presence of God, where they live, work, and play, their redundant reply is, "He's in our church, come hear our pastor," which insinuates God is not where they are.

Those in the church world do not see the Christian life from a real world perspective because it's like "straddling the fence." Christians in the real world see the church world as an exclusive club with self-righteous pompous members, who selfishly interpret Scripture for their advantage. The church world standards seem irrelevant and unrealistic to where they live, work, and play.

CORRECT THEIR FAITH AND THEIR BEHAVIOR WILL FOLLOW!

The Object of Faith
(The Person of the Godhead)

I don't try to (theologically) figure out the orthodox traditional view of the Trinity of Father, Son, and Holy Ghost. It was established at various theological Councils (Synods of Rome-382 A.D) over the centuries under the auspices of the Popes of the Roman Catholic Church authorized by Emperor Constantine. I ascribe to the Godhead concept of God working as One in the world and universe. *"For in Christ all the fullness of the Deity lives in bodily form"* (Colossians 2:9). It doesn't matter "to me" because it doesn't affect my salvation. But the Godhead does because it focuses on the Lord of Glory incarnated as the Messiah, so 'my" faith focus is on the Lord. Hebrews 12:2-3, *"keeping our eyes fixed on Jesus, the pioneer and perfecter of our faith. For the joy set out for him he endured the cross, disregarding its shame, and has taken his seat at the right hand of the throne of God."*

Theologically, concerning the Godhead, we focus on the Person, Nature, and Works of God. There is a four-fold perspective of theology as it relates to the Object of our Faith:

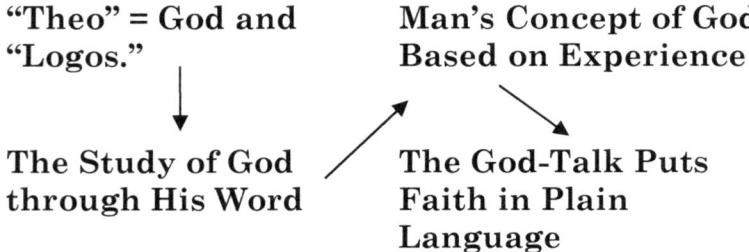

The latter, The God-Talk puts Faith in Plain Language (pragmatic application). That has been my effort writing this book and I hope you can see the practical application of faith. This corresponds to the God-Given Vision that God has disseminated into the Body of Christ that Believers should abide by. That is, the "Great Commission" in their walk of faith, which means winning others for the Lord.

I'll close this book with a **Resuscitation** of the **Effects of a God-Given Image.**

A young man was standing alongside the unbeaten path of a country road. Few people walked or road along that road because it was out of the way of the beaten path where multitudes traveled. ("Enter through the narrow gate. For wide is the gate and broad is the road that leads to destruction, and many enter through it. But small is the gate and narrow the road that leads to life, and only a few find it"—Matthew 7:13-14.). *He was holding a large bundle in his arms because it was his only precious possession and he didn't want to lose it. (When we come to Christ, we don't lose life, we gain life.) An older man came along driving his horse-drawn wagon. The man stopped (Wo), looked at the young man, and said, "Hop on and I will carry you to your destination." The young man obliged the generous offer (The Offer of Redemption) and hopped onto the wagon next to the man. As they proceeded along the road, the older man looked strangely at the young man because he was holding his bundle in his lap. He then said, "I'm carrying you. Why are you still carrying your bundle?"* The moral of the story is in this closing Scripture:

Come to me, all you who are weary and burdened, and I will give you rest.

Take my yoke on you and learn from me, because I am gentle and humble in heart, and you will find rest for your souls.

For my yoke is easy to bear, and my load is not hard to carry. **(Matthew 11:28-30)**

www.ingramcontent.com/pod-product-compliance
Lightning Source LLC
Chambersburg PA
CBHW061737070526
44585CB00024B/2706